How to
Make Your Life
Easier at Work

Al Kelly

Second Edition

McGraw-Hill Book Company

New York   St. Louis   San Francisco   Auckland   Bogotá
Caracas   Colorado Springs   Hamburg   Lisbon
London   Madrid   Mexico   Milan   Montreal
New Delhi   Oklahoma City   Panama   Paris
San Juan   São Paulo   Singapore
Sydney   Tokyo   Toronto

Library of Congress Cataloging-in-Publication Data

Kelly, Al, 1926–
  How to make your life easier at work.

  Rev. ed. of: What to do and what not to do to make
life easier for yourself at work. 1973.
  Includes index.
  1. Success in business.   I. Kelly, Al, 1926–   What
to do and what not to do to make life easier for yourself
at work.   II. Title.
HF5386.K274   1988   650.1   87-29752
 ISBN 0-07-034015-3

 234567890   DOC/DOC   8931098

ISBN 0-07-034015-3

*The editors for this book were William A. Sabin and Jim Bessent, the
designer was Naomi Auerbach, and the production supervisor was
Thomas G. Kowalczyk. This book is set in Baskerville. It was composed
by the McGraw-Hill Book Company Professional & Reference Division
composition unit.*

Printed and bound by R. R. Donnelley & Sons Company.

Contents

Preface

This book is not about the theory of management—it is a practical manual that tells you exactly what to do and how to do it. Leave the theory to the professors of business. You want to do your job in the best and easiest way.

Reading books on management is often an exercise in self-justification, confirming what is wrong with everyone else. The very word "management" implies that we are excellent people who are trying to devise better ways of manipulating and stimulating all our subordinates.

What about managing yourself for a change? How about a detailed examination of all the time-wasting, inefficient things managers do. Take a look at how you organize your time, meetings, correspondence, and at the myriad other aspects of your work that can be radically speeded up and improved.

Plenty of books tell you how so-and-so became president of an international corporation. But you or I may never achieve such eminence—so however amusing, such books are of little value to us in our everyday efforts. We just want to get on to the best of our abilities and enjoy our work. What precisely can a person do *today* and *tomorrow* to achieve that aim? Theory can come later.

This book is for those who like things straight and simple: 8 hours a day for work, 8 hours for sleep, and 8 hours for play, family, and leisure. If you *want* to work 70 hours a week, don't bother reading any further.

No doubt you would like to outstrip your peers, but you want to do it without getting a heart attack in the effort. This book will help you to gain an advantage in every aspect of your work.

Many books on management contain a major fallacy. They give the impression that for the success of a firm, all that is needed is for the CEO to

- Use management style X, Y, or Z
- Decentralize or centralize

- Use this or that management consultant

- Copy the Japanese.

Bunkum.

It's like the golf club captain changing a green or tee just to have something by which to be remembered. It is amusing to look back on the history of many firms which have had a stream of decentralizations and centralizations following each other, all of which claimed to have great beneficial effects.

. You will recognize faults in your own firm and in other firms with which you deal. Don't gloat as you spot the weaknesses of colleagues or your boss. You must try hard to concentrate on your own shortcomings as they unfold. It will hurt because you will not want to change your set ways. But why not give it a try; the relief will be enormous. Just remember, you will not be able to do it all right; otherwise you would be perfect.

The material here is intended both for those just setting out on a career and for those already under way and hoping for promotion. Those at the top can browse and chuckle at how they got most of it correct.

The delicate matter of dealing with people—your boss, subordinates, and colleagues—is spelled out in detail. Management diseases that can strike your business are covered. If you are forewarned about these enemies, you are thus forearmed to ward them off when they attack.

What is said here may not be appreciated by proponents of organization theory or of management by objectives. Nor is it likely to please management consultants or those who cotton to sycophants or the trappings of status.

All of what is written here can be framed around three words: FAIR, FIRM, and FAST. It tells you how to achieve efficiency and how to be effective by applying these three principles in all your activities.

As you read, you may recall similar incidents from your own experience which could well have been included. Your own principles, your likes and dislikes, and your prejudices will come to mind. But there are enough anecdotes and examples here to tease you into changing your wicked ways—if you want to.

Finally, if you read this book, for heaven's sake do not breathe a word about it to your colleagues. Otherwise, they may get it and become as effective as yourself.

Al Kelly
Dublin, 1988

1
It's About Time

Starting Right

Tackle the hardest and most unpalatable jobs first thing in the morning. What a pleasure the rest of the day will be!

- Interview that complainant
- Do that difficult calculation
- Read that long report or specification

The unpalatable task has a knack for getting covered up on the desk. Sure, you intend doing it in five minutes time; but by choosing a simple problem first, you've lost the day's battle. The nasty is often the thing at which you don't excel.

Repeat this rule after lunch. After a while, operating in this way, nothing will daunt you; your confidence will grow and your output will increase. If you pick off the cream first, all those cruel tasks will accumulate. You may be satisfied but other members of your department won't be. And your satisfaction won't last long; the dogs will be yapping at your heels.

As the day progresses, you will delay more and expand on the simple tasks, so that quitting time comes before you can begin that nasty task. Believe it or not, you are ensuring that you can't begin that task. The nearer you get to it, the more desperate you become—making phone calls, going to the loo. You think you are "clearing the decks" but really you are leaving it until tomorrow. Tomorrow never comes.

Don't think that by putting off tough jobs you won't have to do them. They'll be taken on by someone else, or they'll blow up into a crisis. This is the fire brigade approach. Once you get to this state you'll spend all your time putting out fires. You may complain that you're too busy, but it'll be your own doing. What was that about a stitch in time...?

Some Action Guidelines

There's No Time Like the Present

List on a small colored card your tasks outstanding and tick them off as you do them. Make a decision on every single item that reaches you, on the day you get it if you can possibly do that. If not, then put a note on your colored card: "to be attended to as soon as possible." As you finish a task, you cross it off, and you add others as they crop up. Because you use only one card, you will have to transfer any outstanding tasks to a new card every week or two.

On every item of work to be done try to DO IT NOW, not this afternoon or tomorrow. If you devote x minutes the first time you see an item and x minutes the second time, and if the time it takes to do the job is $4x$, you double this by putting it off four times.

Take an average day of 160 three-minute tasks. If you defer each three times, at one minute per deferment, you'll never get through the day's work and you'll get progressively more disorganized and useless. Consider how disastrous this can be. You take twice as long as you should on each item. In two days, you are one day behind. In six months, you are three months behind. In a year, you should be sacked.

If you're in a job where delays will never be noticed and where you have nothing much to do, why on earth are you reading this book?

Don't try to keep the wolves at bay by sending memos or notes promising action later. Back goes the task to the bottom of the pile, to become that much more difficult to tackle. "No hurry," you say, "I wrote about that one a few days ago." (Would you believe two months?)

Don't miss deadlines; otherwise, how can you in all honesty hound others to meet theirs?

If you get a query which has to be answered two weeks from now, don't put it aside. You'll have continually to remember to do it, and it will cross your mind several times in the interim. The date given is the latest date. Occasionally tasks will prove tougher than expected, so give yourself some elbow room.

Hit the Ground Running

Get cracking one minute after you get to the office. The best half-hour's output of work is in this quiet time before the phones start to buzz. It's the best way to prevent an accumulation of work.

Never read a newspaper in the office—unless you're the financial director and have to study *The Wall Street Journal.* There are no ifs, ands, or buts about this. If 16 people read their newspapers for half an hour each morning, you can ban newspaper reading and do without one of them. Everyone knows they shouldn't do this—watch how sheepish they look when you catch them in full scan.

Make It Easy on Yourself

Don't take work home; it will become a disease. You'll stuff all sorts of unpleasant tasks into your briefcase and when you get home, you'll find Johnny has the measles, and then friends will drop in. You'll arrive back in the office with the briefcase unopened, and the merry-go-round begins again. This is escapism. Put nothing in a briefcase—DO IT NOW! Every day is not crisis day, so if you take work home regularly, you're not fit for the job. (In a new job, this rule can be broken for a short spell of a few months.) By the same token, no personal letter writing in the office.

Be at work before, or at least as soon as, your staff every morning, even if you had trouble with punctuality in your youth. If you're not there first, you can't chastise anyone else for being late. It weakens your whole position on malingering of any kind. Who says you can arrive late? You are smug about working late every evening, but it drives your staff mad to see you arrive late when they've been hard at it for a half hour. And so do all those queries you phone them about right at quitting time! You're out of sync; get back in line.

Go home at quitting time. This will force you to get through the day's tasks on time. No 12-hour working days—let alone 14- or 16-hour days. No, let the idiots do that—the bunglers. Worse still is to do it because your boss does. You read the memoirs of presidents of large corporations that do it and demand that all their immediate subordinates do likewise. Their memoirs imply that working long hours equates with success. Well, you'll also see presidents of multinational companies who don't do it. The latter are just more efficient.

Don't let one day's work encroach on the next. This is hard to achieve. As an example, if you are flying back from a meeting, get all your notes organized on the plane. Don't arrive with jumbled notes to be unraveled next day.

Don't arrive to work with a hangover. Life is very short and to go through it in a half stupor is such a waste. Don't let yourself believe that others don't notice; they *do* notice and they *will* talk about it. Bosses fear promoting people who can't take drink in moderation. Of course, drug abuse betrays a similar bent toward self destruction.

To ensure that you organize your private affairs efficiently—thus not

encroaching on your business efficiency—why not list your personal
chores to be done on the back of that same colored card in your pocket.
Knock them off as they're done and have it as a spare memory so you
don't have to worry about forgetting something.

The Telephone

Make your own outgoing calls. Don't ask your secretary to "Get me Mr.
Rasputin please." Now you've got two people trying to get through—
you and your secretary. Expecting the call will just create additional distraction from your other work.

It should be situation normal to have your phone switched to your
desk. This includes internal as well as external lines.

Make it a habit to answer your own phone—even if you have a secretary or share one with others. It's a disgrace to the pin stripes to have
secretaries answering calls all day with "Mr. Smurf's office," "Miss Cab-
bage's phone," and "May I ask who is calling?" What a waste of time! I
find that at least five minutes per day of my own time is wasted by such
delays with inside and outside calls. Imagine it—five minutes a day of
every manager's time in every firm in the world wasted this way, plus
the time of all those secretaries. Junior people are less prone to this
habit—or luxury. They haven't yet attained this level of lunacy. Your
firm could gain 1 percent in time efficiency from all managers if everyone stopped this stupid habit.

Always answer the phone on the first ring. Why wait? Every ring has
you dividing your attention between the phone and what you're trying
to concentrate on. It's like trying to whistle and eat at the same time.

The most efficient managers rarely take longer than a minute on any
phone discussion—about anything.

If another line calls while you are speaking, say "Hold on a moment,
please." Take the other line and say "I'm on another call. Can you
hold?" Usually this caller has only a trifling bit of news and will say
something like "No, I just want to say pork bellies went up 6 cents yesterday." You say "Okay, thanks, that's good." Then you revert to the
first caller, who has been listening to some schmaltzy music on the line
and—I hope—doing some useful work in the five seconds. The first
caller now realizes that another interruption could occur and will expe-
dite the rest of the discussion.

Only when you have an outside visitor should you forward your calls
to your secretary's office. Now here's the problem in reverse: people
who can't pass up a call.

What are you afraid you'll miss by letting your secretary answer the phone when you have a visitor? Who do you think it is, the general manager onto a wrong number, ripe to be impressed by your savvy telephone manner? You've got the "grabbing disease." Even with a visitor in your room you can't let go.

This is discourteous; the caller gets preference over your visitor. Forward your calls to your secretary. If you have no secretary, answer the phone immediately with "Can I ring you back; I've got someone here."

Don't wait to hear half the caller's story. It may be a long one and the storyteller may be bent on finding out who is more important, your visitor or she. If you hear the story out, you insult your visitor. It's a no-win situation. Either way, you end up wasting somebody's time.

In a similar vein, what if the phone rings just as you leave for an appointment? Don't answer it. You'll be late for the appointment, even if you only tell the caller you have no time to talk. Forward the call to your secretary. In the history of business, how many meetings involving how many people have had to wait for one person delayed on the telephone?

And at long last, when you get your other party, don't lapse into a couple of minutes of trivial introductory pleasantries.

"I tried to reach you as soon as I got your message that you were returning my call, but you had gone to lunch."

The longer you delay your real business, the greater the chance of an interruption that will set you back to square one. There you go again.

You should recognize the time waster as soon as you answer the phone. A "white" lie is no harm. "Uh, yes, hello. I'm with some people here just now, but can I help you?"

Don't make excuses. What's the use of telling callers how busy you are:

"There is nobody here today but me and..."

"All our records are all over the place."

"My secretary's out today and I have to answer three phones."

"Can I call you back tomorrow?"

All these were trotted out to me in the course of one day. Consider the impact the total of such conversations has on the national economy, not to mention tying up the telephone exchanges (the telephone company must be ecstatic).

When you phone someone for information and find that person has no idea of the precise problem, don't attempt to educate. Just say "thanks," get off the phone quickly, and phone someone who may know.

Always have your secretary's phone switched over to you whenever he or she is out. This is a marvelous time saver because

- Half the time, the caller is asking if you are free. Say yes.
- The caller may have a bit of information you've been needing. Note it down.
- Time wasters just calling to chew the fat with your secretary will get off the phone fast. "It's okay," they'll say, "I'll ring again."

Where Are You?

Never get lost. Not ever. Never. No. No. No. If you are

- Going to be late
- In another office
- At a conference in Chicago
- Out to lunch

let it be known. Do you know that some callers to your company believe that everyone is perpetually out to lunch? Do you think you can flutter around aimlessly like a butterfly? If you do, people will treat you accordingly.

Silence Is Golden

Will you never shut up! Never talk at length at work about

- Cars
- Sports
- Taxes
- Television programs

A note: Bores who talk on and on about work are no better than golfing or sailing bores, who don't even listen to other enthusiasts! Why, work bores are as bad as baseball or football bores. People don't recognize the failing in themselves. Separately, each complains bitterly about all the other bores, while the rest of us snigger. But how do we know we're not in the same category?

It should rarely be necessary to spend more than five minutes talking to anyone about anything. Remember when you were studying for finals how much you could get through in five minutes? Step up the tempo. I find that discussions that truly deserve more than five minutes—on the telephone or face-to-face—occur only about twice a week.

Why rehash the old days? Nobody is interested in what happened to you 10, 15, or 20 years back. It's the sure sign of a bore. "Why, I can remember when..." It is hardly relevant and the analogies you use to try to demonstrate your knowledge of the new technologies are pathetic to younger technocrats. Better admit your scant knowledge until you can bone up on it (if ever).

People approaching retirement seem to be convinced that development slows down as they close in on 65 and stops thereafter. So after 60 they specialize in "engrossing" younger staff with stories of "how it used to be." Stop it—if you can—and if it's not too late to make any difference to your reputation.

Then you have the bores who are interminably quoting the supposed experts: "I was out to dinner last night with Professor Wrinkly [or Dr. Splotch, or whoever] who says that..." Or they're holding forth on the latest book they've read. And next month it's another book, and you're thinking "Please don't read any more when you finish this one!"

Face to Face

See everyone who wants to see you NOW, not in half an hour or an hour. If you see the person now, you immediately communicate a sense of urgency—she has to grab her stuff and run along at your pace. If you deal with the person now, you won't have that extra appointment cluttering up your memory circuits for the next half hour. A sense of urgency will speed up the discussion and its termination.

Never sit down in anyone else's office when you can avoid it. Standing lends a sense of urgency. If invited to sit down, sit forward on the seat for a quick getaway.

Have no loose chairs near your desk. Put them away behind a table in the corner.

Economize on Talk

Don't apologize for anything you are doing or proposing. Don't say "sorry to bother you" or "sorry to interrupt." If you're truly bothering or interrupting, you shouldn't be. If it's not true, then there's no need padding things out with apologies.

Start at the most recent part of any problem and only go back as far as you must under questioning. This minimizes time usage. You're familiar with the type who goes back to the War of Independence every time he opens his mouth.

Don't belabor a problem. What're you doing? Maybe you intend impressing your audience with its complexity preparatory to offering your coup de grace. They won't be impressed—just watch them fiddle with their pens, or doodle.

Some people complicate a problem so badly that it can't be solved quickly, even if it's a simple question of the office color scheme. This "talent" can land you with "If we pick the green, Ms. Crusty will organize a sit-in; if we pick blue, Mr. Sparkly will resign." Don't mess around with it. Get Sparkly and Crusty in fast. Call the bluff. This and other such "impossible" problems will cease to be put to you. Mr. Sparkly and Ms. Crusty will both "try to be reasonable" and solve the problem for you. It's only hearsay that they harbored such ill will.

Short-Circuiting Long Talkers

Visit Mr. Yakketa in *his* den. That way, it's easier to escape when you've got the information you want. How many times have you thought he was on his way out your door just to have him pop back in again with an addendum to the conversation? His hand was on the doorknob—but he came back. Admit it. Didn't your heart just sink?

Okay. Here's another approach. Let's say Yakketa is due at 11:00. Invite someone else in at 11:10. When your accomplice arrives, invite her in as you say "We are just finished." If you're really desperate, you might consider inviting another person along at 11:15 as added insurance.

Quickly summarize the discussion and agreement or decision when Mr. Yakketa has taken up his quota of your time:

"Right. Very good. We're agreed. You'll produce the sales forecast for the six months concerned by Monday."

"Okay. Here are my staff requirements for the next three years, listed by category. Will you please set down recruitment needs for this period, allowing the normal historical percentage for retirements of any sort."

If you've tried more than one summary and Yakketa is still going full throttle, something more drastic is needed. Excuse yourself and head for the loo, and hope he doesn't follow.

At headquarters, or in any meeting situation, march smartly up to the person you are meeting. If it is someone who usually wastes your time, and if things are getting desperate, here are some remarks you can toss out.

"I don't want to take up too much of your time." (Make sure you're actually in motion when you use this one.)

"I must not keep you from your work."

(Looking at your watch and gasping) "My goodness [or other suitable expletive], I'm late already."

(Catching the eye of one of your colleagues) "I'll be along in a moment, Jane."

Take all the casual chairs out of your office so that Ms. Jabbersmith can't sit down when she descends on you. You know that feeling you get deep within as she sinks into a chair and launches into one of her marathon complications of some issue of little importance.

Arrange offices so that people don't tend to chat. It's not a good thing to have four people in one office if they are engaged in work of a non-repetitive nature. One or two is better. A large number is okay provided you break up the area with potted plants and shrubs, and soundproof it, to turn it into a one-two arrangement.

Making Every Word Pay

Every office has a comedian. Sure, Steve's got a humorous anecdote for every occasion. They *are* funny, but why tell them now, on the job? There is a place for them...off the job. They won't lose their punch.

Never use expressions like (or allow yourself to think that) "Nobody ever tells me anything around here" or "I've never heard that." If you do, you're a whiner. Let's face it, if you're worth telling, if it's not a hopeless waste of time trying to get you to help solve a problem, you'll be told.

Practice leaving gaps in a conversation. It's no virtue to fill every gap unless you're helping substantially to reach a rapid decision. This is a more difficult rule for people reared in a talkative society, but it's worth a try.

When anyone casually joins you and a colleague while you are engaged in a serious business discussion, do NOT NOT NOT say "We were just discussing..." Now you have a third party—with no vital interest in the end result—talking about the thing.

Similarly, try to prevent the size of a meeting from increasing. If two people are discussing something, don't pull in a third. If you need information, call that extra person on the phone, but don't bring him along. Some people think extra people mean a problem will be solved easier or quicker. You know, it's the "two heads are better" theory. But extra people are more likely to unduly prolong the meeting and waste valuable time.

As a corollary—if *you* are the third party, keep your mouth shut no matter how tempting it is to enter the fray. If you believe the result of the debate is crazy, tell the person left with you at the end of the discussion, and leave it to that person.

You know people who spell out about three-quarters of a complicated story and then say they're going to write it up in a memo anyway. The poor slobs must think they've got the toughest job in the world. No wonder, they do everything twice.

Waste no sympathy on those who complicate their own work. They're easy to spot. They're the ones you hear saying things like

"Definitions of responsibility of this group are needed..."

"Someone should have a look at..."

"I am thinking of setting down..."

"We must get someone working on..."

"It will depend on what comes up..."

"The problem has become more complex since last meeting..."

"An in-depth study should be done..."

Making Appointments

Have your secretary make appointments for you on days and at times when you are not busy—and without referring to you. That way, you can group several together and use your time constructively, instead of creating a multitude of interruptions for yourself.

Cram lots of appointments into certain half days, thus making sure that the stream of visitors chase one another along.

If *you* make appointments, always put them in your diary on your desk as you make them so that your secretary will not be confused.

Also, use a simple pocket diary and be prepared to make appointments on the spot. One spread per month is enough to note down all your appointments. Think of it this way: You're only doing one thing at any one time.

It's amusing to hear executives say "I'll consult my diary back at the office." They can't agree to a date on the spot? This makes it unnecessarily difficult to fix a date for anything, because when they get to their offices, they disagree with the date and time tentatively agreed.

So get a very thin pocket diary for $3 and use it to good effect.

Correspondence

Insist that everyone sign and mail their own correspondence with the exception of

- Matters that are out of step with defined company policy (and you'd better define it in all important areas or you can't blame anyone for errors)

- Letters critical of anyone outside your company or any part of your company outside your control

- Anything that, in the judgment of the author, needs to be shown to someone higher up the ladder

The second will ensure that fiery individuals harness their emotions before they send things to you for checking. Releases in the heat of the moment will be eliminated.

The last is very useful. It will identify those who are afraid of their own shadow, as well as the person who never shows anything to anyone and so should be checked on once a year.

Never sign outgoing mail other than your own personal work. If you do, the author is annoyed, the recipient confused, and you are a fraud.

If you want the recipient to know who sent something, TYPE your name below your signature on outgoing mail. Some people seem actually to pride themselves on the illegibility of their signatures.

Don't check the typing of correspondence—just sign it. Let your secretary know this is the rule. In the odd case where an error occurs, don't do anything unless it is of significance. You should, of course, check the typing if it is something going to the president.

Have all incoming mail sorted and sent direct to the person who originated the correspondence. A simple reference system such as PR/JS/1247 ensures that the reply goes straight to Jane Smith in Production on job 1247.

Don't have all queries for all departments under you funneled through you. That's a messenger's job.

Trust your secretary. If you want to open your mail every morning, get a job in the mail room. Have you ever noticed how unimportant 80 percent of your mail is? A good secretary will sift out at least 50 percent of what arrives and send it to whoever deals with such items, or put it in the wastepaper basket.

Altering the work of subordinates in a fussy unnecessary way is like entering an empty restaurant, selecting a table by the window, and having the waiter insist you move to another table. Now do you want to be like that?

Send a telex if you can. In this way the recipient has more time to study the problem and answer fully and accurately. The telex solves the problem of the time difference between Tokyo and New Orleans. Telexes do not require good grammar or syntax. Similarly, you can send sketches or ideas or drafts by facsimile; again, accuracy is not paramount and handwriting will suffice.

Be Considerate

Make your letters short and to the point. I've been accused of writing nothing but one-sentence memos.

If you ever revise a report or document, always note the changes you made so that the unfortunate recipient doesn't have to read it all again. How I wish people would do this! If the people you work with do not do this, ask them to please do it.

Assume that the recipient is intelligent and knows what to do. Don't bother referring to previous notes or spelling out that it is the "gross turnover, less tax to be taken at 3 percent on all revenue jobs." Come on, that's what it has always been.

Such short notes make some managers nervous. Don't be surprised if someone calls asking you "just to clarify if it is the gross turnover, less tax…." Just say "That's right Watson, as always. I can always count on you to get things straight right off." They'll pick up on the sarcasm eventually.

You can launch the most difficult and serious matters in the same way:

"Please examine the technical feasibility and economics of a frequency recovery relay system for 60 percent of loads in this electric utility and report by July 1st next."

Now here's a project that calls for extensive design work and the economic impact is very far-reaching. So what? Three lines says it. Why write two pages?

Don't write a letter in reply unless it is necessary to keep the original. Write a brief answer on the end of the incoming letter and mail it back to the sender. This isn't rude; it's practiced by many large organizations on their external correspondence.

Remember what Dean Acheson said: "People write memoranda not to give information but to put someone in his place." Think about this. If you want to give some good news to a colleague, you will phone.

"I have the very person you want for that job."

"I can help you cut your budget."

But if you want to put people in their place, what do you do? You write...no, you compose...a memorandum. Such notes are long and carefully constructed, and grammatical (to bolster the argument). Whenever I see a two-page memo arriving, I know before I read it that someone is griping, quoting company policy, and/or exposing some area in which I have exceeded authority.

Incidentally, such notes are frequently issued just before the author disappears on a trip or takes a vacation—so that you can't hit back. And to rub salt into the wound, copies are sent to six colleagues...and the boss!

Handling Representatives

See only those representatives that you alone should see, and who offer something you really need. Never see a representative because her company sent you, or may send you, a Christmas gift or an invitation to dinner. Never see a representative just because you did business with him in a previous, junior post. This smacks of cronyism.

Don't lunch with a calling representative unless you have been working together all morning and will be working all afternoon. Chances are you'll be asleep from too much food and gin by about 3 p.m. Even if you are to work with the rep later in the day, make some good excuse to skip lunch (for the personality that repays with interesting conversation, it's all right to occasionally break this rule). I find that the caller is just as pleased to avoid a large meal in the middle of the day. A rep's job is unhealthy. They die young from overeating and overdrinking. Give them a break and do yourself a favor at the same time.

All Meetings Great and Small

Command Meetings: When, Why, and How

Meet those reporting direct to you regularly—every four to eight weeks—with a formal agenda. This produces team effort and makes sure that everyone appreciates the group's activities and problems.

These are command meetings, in which you will have to rule on anything not agreed on by all.

Are you afraid of meeting those reporting to you at regular sessions? Those who are afraid usually argue that they see their subordinates regularly anyway, so why gather them together? Sure, you may lose face occasionally because two or three of them will get together and beat you over the head on something about which you haven't a clue, but look how essential that is.

At command meetings, tasks are handed out for the next reporting period. Give yourself a fair share, and get all yours done in double-quick time. Your tasks should be those that can't reasonably be done by anyone else.

Set a time limit for command meetings—an hour is sufficient 95 percent of the time—and stick to it. If it goes any longer, the time will be taken by people not reporting results but trying to work problems out in public. A very useful rule is to limit each person to five minutes (maximum) to give a rundown on progress. If one cannot do it in five minutes, then force the issue, cut it off, do something—because the others who did hold it to five minutes are going to be smoldering inside.

Insist on similar command meetings lower down the line at regular intervals, run by managers in each group—with agenda and minutes. Sit in occasionally, when things are on target, to find out how it is being done. Sit in regularly when things are critical or not going well. If the problem spot is far away geographically, don't miss a meeting for that reason. Your presence makes for extra effort to impress. It's as simple as that. The rivalry to produce the goods at such meetings will help the job along enormously. It's amazing what gets done in the hour before a command meeting.

Why not encourage some of your subordinates to meet without you? If you have three production managers reporting to you—as well as four other departments—then it is a good idea that the production managers meet without you periodically. I've seen such meetings banned in firms where it was feared that these caucus meetings would undermine management's authority. Could it be the fear that the management's shortcomings would be discussed and attacked? Certainly such managers have much in common and can

- Develop a standardized reporting scheme
- Devise solutions and recognize common problems

Such meetings will prevent friction and suspicion developing between them.

Insist on similar command meetings higher up the line which you should attend. If not held, pester till you get them. Remember that the flow of commands and information up, down, and across occurs best when organized in this formal way.

The "Quickie"

If you want a quick meeting, be there one minute before the due time. If you're able to arrive 15 minutes early, you should be doing more useful work elsewhere. Never be late, however.

Don't put off the fixed date and time even if you have to skip something that sounds interesting. Such postponements are a reflection of a manager's belief that his or her time is more important than those inconvenienced.

If you set a starting time late, late in the morning, you intimate that the meeting must end preferably by noon, no later than 12:30.

Don't think you're required to lecture on every topic because you are sitting at the head of the table. The effectiveness of chairpersons is measured not in how much of the discussion they monopolize, but in how much listening they do and how many decisions they make. It's astonishing the way perfectly meek committee members blossom into such colossal bores once they take the chair.

Don't be late. If you arrive late to chair a meeting it will lead to

- Someone else carrying on until you arrive

- Your asking "How far did you get?" and then having the meeting go back over the whole agenda to see what was decided

- You adding your own comments and the whole meeting having to start afresh

Working Meetings

It's a good plan to decide in advance on the points you wish to make for any meeting or important phone call and to jot them down on a pad. In this way you can ensure that the meeting or phone call is efficiently used and that you do not forget the necessary points.

Have an agenda circulated beforehand, not one day, but three or four days beforehand. Don't use some obsolete agenda with general headings that have long since lost their meaning, like

- Production
- Distribution

- Sales

Rubbish!

Don't arrive laden down with files, books, pens, and papers. It conveys confusion and lack of a positive system. Homework for meetings should be done *before* you leave your office.

If the other participants don't have all the data they need, don't hang around. Set a time and venue for another meeting and get out. Otherwise you risk ending up working out their data for them.

In a working party, it is a good plan not to let the most senior person take the chair. He or she will then act only as chairman to sum up the discussion and enumerate the decisions reached. The meeting will turn out to be a command meeting, whereas all members should be actively doing some work.

Say the minimum and NEVER NEVER NEVER hog the conversation. Listen to the point of view of others and when you do talk, you'll command attention and respect. To see the truth of this, consider those whose opinion you respect, and think how little they talk at meetings. Try to speak for half the length of time taken by the next least loquacious person present.

If you talk too much at meetings, the others will be thinking up clever contributions they'll make as soon as you dry up. They'll only half listen to your meanderings. The meeting becomes a chess game, with each protagonist more interested in the second next move than the current one.

Shorten the meeting by agreeing with anyone tending to reach a quick, sensible solution, rather than taking issue with those going off on tangents. Leave them there to return if they please. Fight the temptation to pursue Alice into Wonderland or you'll end up getting lost too.

Decisions can be reached on a basis of 99 to 1 (virtual unanimity), or 51 to 49 (virtual deadlock). If you see it as 49 to 51, there is little point spending time pushing the difference of two. But if it stands at 25 to 75, the difference is too great to be a matter of opinion. Some facts are missing, so get someone to supply them.

If the meeting is held in your office, at the conclusion get to your desk and onto the phone. This should prevent stragglers from hanging on for a chat.

If you are going to a meeting called by someone else and you know it will be boring, bring some work with you and some blank paper. Thus you can get through lots of work while others at the meeting will marvel at your interest in the proceedings.

One exception is meetings with union officials, which often continue through the lunch hour, so don't start them too early. Union officials need to report back on protracted negotiations through meal breaks, so respect these arrangements.

The Devil Disguised as a Meeting

Many times when you want to talk to someone that person is "at a meeting." How often are you at a meeting when others are looking for you? Some meetings are necessary and good. Many (most?) are useless.

The disease of calling meetings is usually to be found in particular parts of an organization. The personnel or planning sections are notorious for "calling meetings." In a way, it's natural for them to do so because they

- Are not "in-line" management
- Have time on their hands
- Cannot then be accused of not consulting all interests

How do you control the impact of this disease? It's easy. Don't go to such meetings.

First, insist that a note be sent to you before any meeting on any topic is held. When you get this note, write on the margin your views and send back a copy the day you get it. If you write "I agree," then you can justifiably stay away from the meeting.

If all else fails—send a very junior representative so that the convenor will see how unimportant you consider the meeting to be. After a while word will get around that it is useless inviting you to meetings.

People with courage are reluctant to call meetings. They go ahead and do their job without having innumerable meetings trying to get everyone to agree on what should be done.

It could be argued that a proper organization would reduce the necessity for meetings. Not so. Every timid manager finds a reason for consulting finance, production, operations, personnel, maintenance, and sales before moving. The brave manager forges ahead. She may send a copy of the final plan to some or all of those concerned with a note saying something like "Any serious imperfections should be brought to my attention by the end of the present month." Nothing will come back.

Fast, Accurate, and Useful Minutes

Write the minutes at the meeting. Hand them in for typing on the way back to your office. If necessary, prolong the meeting by three minutes or so to do this. You'll save the time you would spend writing beautiful prose a week or a month later. Better to settle for poor style today.

For years, I admired individuals who were doing this, convinced that such talent was rare. Eventually, when I moved into a new post, I tried it. The relief was enormous. Instead of arriving back at the office laden down with ten pages of notes, I handed over eight pages of minutes.

If you think it's a chore getting minutes written at the meeting, wait and see how excited you are about it when you arrive back at your desk and find all those messages waiting for you. Also, recording something you've talked about at length is dull and you will seize the slightest excuse to delay.

Get the minutes circulated quickly. They are supposed to summarize the prior proceedings, not serve exclusively as the agenda for the subsequent meeting. Minutes that come out a day before the next meeting are useless. Then, everyone is busy making their own notes to remind themselves of what they must do. When they know they can trust your record, the meeting speeds up because the scribbling stops.

This writing of minutes has another virtue: It gives an excuse to stop the conversation from wandering. You can butt in with "Well, ladies and gentlemen, is it okay to minute this discussion like this?" This should stop splinter groups from going off on side-issue discussions.

Identify in the margin of all command meeting minutes

   X For action by you before the next meeting

  XX For action by the divisional head before the next meeting

XXX For action by the departmental manager before the next meeting

Don't make notes of tittle tattle. The participants will wonder if it is to be used as evidence in court at a later stage. Set dates for everything and minute them for all to see.

If you are not the person recording the minutes, as soon as anything is decided requiring action by you, don't make a note reminding yourself to write to Spiro asking for the facts. Write the letter to Spiro on the spot. This will help to

- Keep the letter short, because you have to pay attention to the proceedings

• Get quick action, because you can give your script in for typing on the way back to your office

Committees: In-Company and Out

One Head Is Often Better Than Two or More

Setting up a committee to examine a specific problem sounds sensible. But look what happens: The committee will find it difficult to hold meetings. An agreed work program will take up two meetings. In a year they have their report together...maybe.

Consider an alternative method. Give one person the task. Now the work program is written in an hour and the study is finished in a few weeks. Better still, this person can go ahead and begin implementing the results, whereas the committee merely says what should be done.

Take a practical example. A committee is set up when a glaring problem exists—such as failure of machinery that has been installed worldwide.

The committee would probably set off en masse to look at many machines because some members of the committee would not have been familiar with them. Indeed, committees are usually "broad-based," which basically means that some of the representatives have zero familiarity with the technicalities of the task assigned. A year later, they would report the same thing that the person working alone could do in a few days—and now you would still have to appoint the one person to do something about it!

Have no in-company committees—command meetings yes—working parties yes—but *no* committees. Otherwise, no one person is responsible for the outcome and you will get the mess you deserve. If you want to stop anything from happening or put off making an unpleasant decision, a committee is useful. But a committee cannot control or build anything.

Occasionally, you may have a small (two to three persons) working party reporting by a set date on a specific problem, but remember that decision making rests with the manager calling for the report, not with the working party.

Governments regularly set up committees to investigate problems. They do this so that a year or two can pass before anything need be done—and the next election is due just then.

One committee, after a year's work, reported that instead of doing what it was set up to do, it proposed to examine an entirely unrelated topic. There were some quite able persons involved, but a year is a long time and they simply avoided attending in the end, while the dregs of the committee gradually went off the rails.

I have seen committees that were effective, but when I checked up I found that one person did all the work, made all the decisions, and wrote up the results, which the committee gladly endorsed as its findings. It could have been finished in one-tenth of the time but for the formality of getting at least a decent number of meetings held. The drones love committees for the reflected glory. Don't give them the chance. Give the task to the one person who can and will do the job.

The extreme case of absurdity is a "committee" which meets to exchange views on the inadequacy of staff and budget to produce desired results.

Committees are self-perpetuating. They usually end their voluminous reports by pointing out further tasks to be done, for example

- In-depth study of plant management
- A study of the adequacy of resources
- A study on the desirability of further subcommittees

All are beautifully vague aims which would in time lead to the generation of further aims of the same sort.

Formal, Organized Nonaction

Never, never set up a committee (even if you call it a working party) to examine and report on any aspect of your organization. It will produce a very large report between beautiful covers, with a small window through which you can see some impressive title, such as *Technology Development Study*.

When it is done, the report will surely be "presented" to you and others, complete with slides in three colors, with conclusions and recommendations and action dates. But what will such a committee recommend? The members will tend to be kind to existing institutions and pockets of inactivity. They will be "nice chaps"; every single expansionist request or idea will be incorporated without too much of a challenge. Nothing will be quantified. The certainty of divine retribution will be forecast if the report's recommendations are not heeded.

The report will also manage to show a few new promotional posts—never the removal of any deadwood. Nobody on the committee has individual responsibility for the budget involved in the organizational unit being examined—so why should they recommend economy.

Pity any group not represented on such a committee. There is nobody to defend them. So they will not get any of the promotions or extra staff. It's like the Republicans being in power. They're not going to bother themselves to give jobs to the Democrats.

Don't sit on more than two committees outside your job at any time. This includes golf clubs, social clubs, and professional associations. If you do, you are likely to become a professional committeeperson. You'll grow dangerously accustomed to the indecision and blather. Such committees off the job are harmless, of course. The work is all done by one person usually. But they may give you bad habits.

Committees are an exercise in exhibitionism. Each participant gets to prance about showing off some fancy steps for all to see—and have it recorded in the minutes.

The greatest insult I can imagine is "There goes a great committee man."

The Lowest Common Denominator

If two people are discussing what to do about a problem, the emerging consensus must be what they both think is appropriate, that is, the lowest common denominator of the ideas they can muster. If you have five persons involved in the decision, then the consensus will be far more conservative because any brave or innovative ideas will not be common to the five. This explains why a committee can never innovate or move quickly. On the other hand, it will not allow mistakes because some member will throw up an objection to any given possibility. So if you want caution, delay, snail-pace development, and no errors, then set up your committee. Otherwise, don't.

Other companies or states or even countries may appear more efficient than you. But if you do business there, you may be appalled to see the myriad meetings going on all day and late into the night, all because nobody wants to make a decision, or take responsibility.

Conferences: A National and International Plague

When you attend a large business conference, do you tell the truth when you meet another delegate in the foyer, while other delegates are in listening to papers in six different auditoriums?

"How are you enjoying the conference?" she asks.

Do you say that

- Ninety percent of these papers say nothing more than that milk is white.

- Most of the speakers have diagrams that cannot be read by the audience. They mumble rather than speak distinctly (except manufacturer's sales representatives who must get it right or lose their job). The only value gained is from casual meetings in the hall in which you compare notes, off the record, on things you dare not mention in a lecture (lest the manufacturer, whose miserable service record you would dearly love to expose, should choose to litigate). Who wants to have their shameful errors broadcast? But wouldn't it be of immense value in avoiding similar disasters for all of us to know these kinds of things?

Manufacturers must attend these conferences as a marketing exercise, so a crowd is guaranteed. Your firm must, from fear, send someone, or they will appear backward.

When you go home, you tell the boss how wonderful the conference was and all the useful things you learned. Don't worry. The boss sent you as a sort of bonus or prize—a day off—for working well last year and knows well what such events are all about!

Multilingual conferences are a menace, hundreds of delegates cooped up in theaters listening to simultaneous translations of lectures. The joke is that each delegate, through earphones, has to listen to a multitude of very odd translations.

I once jotted down the following in one eight-minute session at a conference in France:

"...circumscribe the possible solutions favorably available..."

"...depend on the wide influences of the restraining affecting factors..."

"...on the basis of the conceptual acceptance of the regimes which are incidentally accidental..."

"...the devices which are disarmed of the affections..."

And there were 6000 delegates! Do any of these passages mean anything to you?

Writing down this nonsense—so that I could lampoon it later on—was the only value I gleaned from the session. So, be very selective about attending such conferences. Better to read the papers in good translations. Many conferences simply rehash previously published papers to keep a company name before the public.

Some worldwide organizations deliberately add momentum to the conference-holding contagion, employing staff just to generate lecture sessions, the income from which will pay for their services.

I once met a professor who had not been back in his home country for seven months. He'd been away attending bloody conferences. I wonder if anyone missed him?

Papers presented by many authors seem to consist of vague circumlocutions with no definite information on anything—and this even before the interpreter mistranslates it. Whew! Be selective, very selective, with time-wasting conferences.

Clamp down on applications for staff to attend that conference in Miami or the one in Hawaii. The argument usually put forth as rationalization for attendance is "to keep up-to-date on my specialty." Have they suddenly become illiterate? Let them write for the published proceedings and papers if this is essential information. Why must they hear it from the horse's mouth? Only those who can genuinely contribute to the advancement of a given field should attend.

Be very suspicious of conferences on vague topics such as

- Public relations
- Communications
- Absenteeism

I was cajoled into presenting a paper at an international conference on public relations in Berlin. You could not make out the slides shown by most speakers. They spoke too rapidly. What they had to say consisted primarily of useless platitudes. How had we made it all those years without such late-breaking advice as

"Keep your plant in good repair."

"Do not exceed recommended temperature limits."

"Monitor and record all salient figures."

Am I being unfair? Am I? I don't think so. I even feel guilty about my own effort.

This extends as well to the resolutions of such groups as the European Communities where the Council publishes such gems as

"Keep oil imports from third countries within reasonable proportions."

"Each member state and the Community should continue to rely on an appropriate combination of policy measures and the operation of market forces."

All of that was in one three-page official publication to be distributed all over the world and, presumably, to be read and digested by thousands of people. What a waste of time and effort. If the leaders of our various entities—nations, businesses, whatever—cannot make wise decisions, such empty words certainly will not help them get it right.

But then it gives employment to a lot of people who produce such reports. That's an advantage of sorts, isn't it? I'm being facetious.

Cardinal Rules of Chapter 1

DO	DON'T
Tackle the most difficult task first	Take work home
List tasks to be done	See all incoming or outgoing post
Take your own incoming telephone calls	Get lost
Stop talking so much	Swap yarns at work
Be on time	Burden yourself with committees
Avoid Mr. Yakketa	Postpone any meeting
Hold short command meetings monthly	Attend useless meetings called by someone else
Write minutes at every meeting	See representatives or have lunches that can be avoided
Give a task to one person	Attend useless conferences
In minutes of meetings record specific tasks and their deadline dates	
Agree with others wherever you can to speed up meetings	

2

The Well-Oiled Machine

Get Organized

The major difference between a good and a poor performer is how a person organizes the working day. Did you ever wonder why Napoleon and Julius Caesar were able to do as much as they did? Tremendous organizing ability was a key factor.

You can prove this to yourself as follows: Select a subordinate who is not producing sufficiently. Go through all the work that employee should have done by now, item by item. In each case just ask "What do you think should be done about this item?" and jot down the response on a sheet of paper—without giving your own opinions. The whole exercise could take as little as a half hour.

Having gone through all the outstanding work you will find that all the answers are correct. So why has this employee not done the work to which she knows all the solutions? You may well ask.

Ironically, the person subjected to this examination will resent your investigation because it makes her appear foolish. But you should ask that the work be done as outlined and repeat the same exercise in a month to try to get that poor performer to improve. Tell her that life is a long distance race and that all past inefficiencies disappear into oblivion when efficient work takes over.

So get organized and get your people organized.

Concentrate

Don't read anything twice—not a word or a line or a sentence. Train yourself to concentrate on what you're doing, not on baseball, or your family, or even other aspects of your job, when reading a specific item. Avoid the "Joycean" thought process—thinking simultaneously of forty different things as you skim through your correspondence. Otherwise, you'll find you've reached the end without getting the full import. Remember your school days: READ THE QUESTION! READ THE QUESTION! READ THE QUESTION!

Some people spend much of their working day dawdling:

- Daydreaming
- Looking out the window
- Putting heaps of papers in tidy bundles
- Making up their T&E's
- Doodling
- Always about to do something

You cannot concentrate all the time, but try to keep the dawdling to a manageable minimum.

Incoming Mail

A pile arrives in the morning. How should you tackle it? If you have organized properly (as described in Chapter 1), what arrives on your desk can only be done by you. So set quickly about doing it!

While every item must be dealt with today, it is allowable to sift through quickly, pulling out items for really fast action—a simple "yes" or "no" scribbled by you for your secretary to handle. You will be left with the really important items. Select and deal with the most difficult one first (see the first sentence of this book) and then tackle the others.

This may sound impossible, but consider what arrives on a typical day:

Item: Things for approval at your level in the organization (filling a vacancy, a promotion for which interviews have been held, payment to a supplier).

Action: Read quickly, sign, and put in your OUT tray.

Item: Trade magazines.

Action: Scan the index and read only the articles of current direct interest. Throw away those that your company library will have. Send others to a subordinate. Do not attempt to synopsize an article for anyone else.

Item: A report; for example, one proposing a reorganization in a branch office.

Action: You should already know the real reason why this reorganization is proposed. Phone the author and discuss the details. Then return the lot with other minor comments on a slip attached.

You should be able to read and deal with all correspondence in under an hour. On most days a half hour should suffice. Otherwise you're simply reading what others are doing and leaving yourself no time for your own job.

Don't handle any piece of paper twice. Never read what others should have received if it arrives by mistake on your desk. It may be darned interesting but resist the temptation and put it in the out tray for the right person. If you read it, you will think about it, talk about it, or—worst of all—maybe even try to do something about it. It's just one more unnecessary distraction.

For Your Eyes Only

"Confidential" is the sort of item your secretary can deal with for you and sign the reply. It's probably from the personnel department anyway.

"Private and confidential" is the same as confidential; it's just that the sender is a bit younger and is experiencing delusions of being a secret agent.

If there is something so sacred that only your privileged eyes should see, it will be sent over by a runner. This may happen once in two years.

Could You Put That in Writing, Please

You have listed on a small colored card—which you keep in your pocket—the things you have to do soon, both at work and at home, with work items on one side and domestic chores on the other. As you finish them, you cross them off, and you add others as they crop up. Because you use one card, you have to transfer the outstanding ones to a new card every week or two. For example:

Item: "Visit Santa Monica." Uh, oh. That operation is not up to snuff and you must go there today and go through the operating figures to see what you can suggest. Fix on 3 o'clock to be there.

Item: You saw that one plant had considerably reduced downtime by using a gadget called Turnite. Write to all plant managers telling them this.

If you don't write them down, you will get into all sorts of trouble. Take an example from your private life. You have a term paper your niece sent you to read a few weeks back. You were to comment on it (she respects your judgment) and return it promptly, because she needs it for gaining admission to a certain college. If you fail to send it back in time, you'll be blamed for ruining her entire future. And if you don't write it down, you might forget you have it. Get the picture?

Trick yourself if you have to—put the paper in your coat pocket, or on the car seat, or in your briefcase, now, so that in your early-morning grog state you can't walk out without it. Don't trust yourself. Try to make it impossible to go wrong.

To Read or Not to Read

Don't waste your time reading economic forecast letters. There are several prestigious ones addressed only to presidents and chairpersons of large firms. So anyone who reads them is enabled to entertain the delusion of perhaps becoming president of the firm. You have only to read one carefully to see that George Bernard Shaw was right when he lamented the proneness of economists never to commit to one straightforward position. These letters always forecast what will happen "on the one hand" and "on the other hand," so they can always refer back selectively to their "correct" analysis.

Every schoolchild knows the two sides of such questions. Why commit it to mauve-colored paper and entitle it *The Bunkum Circular*, even if it is the best vehicle for honoring the Noble Price Winner in Economics, P. Ure Bunkum.

Reading *Time* or *Newsweek* on airplanes will tell you most of what you need to know about such questions—and it's free. It is boring reading magazines on subscription; you feel you have to read the whole issue. But on a plane you're trapped for a definite, but limited, period of time and can therefore afford to be selective and just read the one item of direct value to you.

The Value of Scintillating Prose

Get in the habit of doing every writing job once only...no revising, no editing, no polishing. It's not worth it, and if you know there is to be no revising, it'll improve your concentration.

Don't make even second drafts of minutes, agendas, letters, memos.

This only doubles the work. So what if it's not perfect? If it's sufficiently bad, someone will howl. In practice, this will happen rarely, say 0.01 percent of the time, so why do 200 percent to avoid that?

Do You Gotta One-Track Mind?

If you handle only one problem at a time, you'll become a blinkered horse. The laser-beam mind, while impressive, is useless unless you are on a single research project with no deadline and no budget limit. People will forget you exist and the problem you're tackling will be forgotten as well, or will be done quickly by someone else. So keep several pots boiling and stir them all regularly.

If you have 20 current problems, give each a nudge often. The cook who can simmer soup, boil potatoes, roast beef, make gravy, steam vegetables, bake a pudding, whip the cream, and percolate the coffee—without burning, boiling over, or drying up anything—is the winner. If you can do it at home, you can do it in the office.

Lightening Your Load

Sit down at least once a year, say, just after Christmas, and

- Review what it was that took up so much of your time. Can any one general rule or procedure be devised to avoid some specific set of tasks? If so, make the rule or go and seek agreement to it. Accumulate examples and battle to get the rule accepted. One hard day's work now will save many over the next year. Never continue making repetitive decisions. Instead, make one decision and record that in future you only want to see items that are exceptions to that decision.

- Check on what regularly arrived in your morning post that was not your concern, for example, magazines and literature that you readdressed to someone else. Get them deflected at the source.

- Write notes of praise to those who have recently deserved them.

A note in your bring-forward (BF) file will remind you to do this.

Keep on Top of Things

Check the minutes of the last command meeting (see Chapter 1) and have a standing instruction with your secretary to launch volleys on anything you are to attend to (everything marked X), and to mark in red on your copy of the minutes those things that you must do. You can then personally wrap it up by closing time. In this way you do the least possible amount yourself.

Keep a BF file in which an extra copy of items of importance is lodged. Then, once a month your secretary will plant the file on your desk (and you must sign that you did peruse it). You have to keep this file thin, so anything that has not yet been acted upon gets a reminder. The reminder can just be something like "Status?" Be sure to put the date.

This BF system is the sweeper that keeps the laggards moving. You do not have to worry that you have forgotten anything of importance. The file serves as your memory.

Reading Between the Lines

Do not beg any questions in any report going to your boss or the board of your company. For example,

- "In the next report a final estimate of the cost will be submitted." A statement like this will terrify the board into thinking that there is a 5 percent cost overrun, whereas you merely mean that the figures are not completed but there will be no further need for dollars. So either say nothing or say that no further cash will be needed.
- If a project is overexpended by $16,000, you must not leave the statement hanging in mid air, begging such queries as "What percentage is that of the total project cost, 50 percent or 0.001 percent?"

Do not say, with six months to go, that the new central computer will be working on the 16th of September. That is being unnecessarily specific. Say that, as promised initially two years ago, the computer will be working in September. In the first case, you may have to explain why it came in on the 20th. In the latter, you never aimed at other than September, so there's nothing to explain.

In large reports that arrive to you, look not only at the conclusions or arguments. Focus particularly on what is not included or argued. If a report fails in its basic assumptions, it is useless to read the rest.

Take an example of a report on selling coal to certain industries. If the report bases its whole argument on a statement that industry needs coal of certain sizes, check that out by calling two people in two industries to see if the sizes quoted in the report are right. Do not be surprised if you find that the industries you contact can in fact use other sizes without any extra cost.

The reason such reports make basic errors in their assumptions is that they are often based on general textbook information. This seems to give a scientific basis for the conclusion of the report. Such generalized figures are of little use in a particular problem in the business world. Far more detailed information is needed. Don't be afraid to question conclusions. They're not sacred.

On Being a Packrat

Your job is management. Don't let your office, or any area you are responsible for, become a storage facility—unless, of course, you are managing a warehouse. Keep your office tidy and uncluttered: no old calendars on the wall (even if you like the picture), no college notebooks, no magazines you piously intend to get around to reading one fine day, no rough notes taken at meetings, nothing that belonged to your predecessor in the office. If the calendar is out of date, throw it out. Use your desk calendar or pocket diary.

Jettison papers at every opportunity:

- In hotel wastepaper baskets
- At airports
- In airplanes
- Immediately after meetings

Keep nothing that can be got somewhere else should you want it (face it, you never will).

If you feel like you're violating the freedom of the press to discard any printed page, then forward them to some of your less liberal colleagues in the company. They'll dispose of them without blinking an eye.

It's a mistake to keep large bookshelves in your office. They will fill up with useless stuff that will be thrown out on the day you retire. Beat them to it and let the company benefit from the value of your waste paper.

Even worse is the bookcase with a glass front, which makes you feel obliged to fill it with rows of impressive looking tomes. Most of us need little more than a 3-foot-wide shelf. Any book that you haven't used in the past six months should go to the company library, even if you bought it yourself.

I've known people who retired before they threw away their college notes. (I kept some of my own for 20 years before dumping them—reluctantly, unused—in the wastepaper basket. I had coped with problems far more complex than the ones covered in the notes.)

You need a shallow drawer that locks for work that is yet to be completed. Don't put any outstanding work elsewhere. You will be amazed how you will have to get rid of the rubbish. It used to be said that if you keep something seven years, you will find a use for it. But is it worth waiting seven years? Who knows where things will stand seven years hence? You may not be there by then (you hope).

Don't keep anything on your desk other than papers collected for tomorrow's meeting or awaiting specifically requested data for work in which you personally are involved (and no one else).

But don't be fooled. The person who has an uncluttered room and a clear desk may be either of two types:

- Very efficient, with all incoming work done, planning some improvement in technique
- Lazy and inefficient, hoping that a huge backlog of work hidden in the drawer will somehow go away

Which are you?

Avoid an in-basket where paperwork stacks up. This is the "deep-litter" system, if you know what I mean. It produces excellent fertilizer, but it'll kill you. Spend two minutes fifteen times a day searching the litter for an item and your time is gone up in smoke. An extreme case is the person with a cabinet chock full of papers, all awaiting decisions. I knew one so full you couldn't open the doors without causing an avalanche. Whenever I see someone putting papers into a drawer during the day, I get a sinking feeling they are being left there to ferment.

You don't need an in-basket or box. Just let items arrive on the desk and deal with them at once.

Maybe you are one of those magazine or report hoarders. You are going to read them, soon...tomorrow! Right? Wrong. You never will. Read them now, or send them to the library or to someone whose purpose it is to keep such things, or put them in the wastepaper basket. A good rule is to do this exercise the afternoon before holidays—at Christmas, Easter, summer vacation—and dump 50 percent of everything in the room. You've met the sort of person I mean, peering from behind a barricade of journals: "I'm going to read them when I get time." The fact that he mentions them reveals his guilt complex.

Don't keep drawers full of papers that should be in the files. You're keeping them at your fingertips just in case you want them. Right? You never will. Besides, when you're away, your boss and colleagues can't find anything. They don't like this. You don't seem indispensable, just confused. Trust the filing system you've got until you get the chance to improve on it.

Do not order another filing cabinet because your existing one is full. Instead, purge the existing one, one file at a time. Throw away at least 50 percent of what has been there for under six months and 90 percent of all before that. Make up your mind that you'll clean out at least three or four files a day. Put them on your desk each afternoon when you leave, and tackle them first thing the next morning. You should have no more than 50 or 60 files, so the lot will be done in three weeks or so. You will find that whatever you threw away when last you decimated the file was never needed in the meantime. How often have you had to go elsewhere looking for a copy of what you threw away? It has never happened to me.

Take, for example, your file on budgets. Once a year you get submissions from which you make your budget for the year. Once made and approved, you could (after a decent interval of, say, two months) dump all the submissions. If ever you needed a look, which is unlikely, you could ask for the one item of interest.

Do not file the copy of a memorandum addressed to someone else that comes to you from within the company. This is because the originator has it filed. The copy was sent to you so that you would know it was sent and be aware of the contents. Rely on your memory; trust it. If it is important, you will remember it. If it is unimportant, the sooner you forget it the better.

A Workable Filing System

Amazingly, one thing that seems to beat the ingenuity of many is the design of a good filing system. I've encountered total confusion on three continents. Design is perhaps too grand a title. I have been lucky in that I arrived in a design office at 23 years of age where a filing system existed which has been used successfully and copied copiously. It goes like this.

The firm is divided into departments, so the first initial on the file represents the department, for example, P for Production. The second denotes the job; for example, Lx is Lexington Project. The next is a number depicting the actual file on that job; 16 could be the civil engineering file.

P/Lx/16/TP

The last two letters tell the name of the person doing that work. TP, for example, might be Thomasina Papadopoulos.

It's a marvel of simplicity:

- All correspondence coming in goes straight to TP.
- Any filing to be done gets put straight into file No. 16 in the filing cabinet drawer for Lexington.

It's a system that well suits an office where a lot of people use the files.

Another simple system used by a single manager who keeps a set of files is as follows. Use an alphabetical list for all the areas in use. A new file can easily be inserted at any time, or one thrown away when there is no longer any use for it:

Abilene Project

Budgets

Correspondence with Personnel Department

Such a system works. Anything being filed need not have any reference written on it. You know where to put it and where to look. Some few items can have a copy in a second file if they refer to two items.

There is no need for an elaborate coding system for filing. Such a system ensures confusion and difficulty. Why use symbols that are longer or more vague than the thing symbolized? Nobody can remember what all those numbers and hyphens and decimals mean.

In Quest of the Super Secretary

The selection of a secretary is one of the most important tasks any manager faces. Here's where research on the candidates will pay off. Check to see which

- Has the highest output
- Can innovate
- Takes responsibility
- Is 100 percent accurate and can correct all your poor syntax and grammar
- Is cool under pressure
- Can set up and operate all sorts of control systems (filing, reminder system, collecting reports by due date)
- Is polite to callers and managers

Don't settle for a candidate who "is adequate" or "does well enough." Be selfish. Your whole output and efficiency depend heavily on that secretary.

Dictate to a shorthand writer only at a time when you get no interruptions—the first half-hour of the day, while the bums are slurping their coffee and reading their newspapers.

But don't dictate at all unless it is absolutely necessary. If "yes" or "no" or "next Tuesday" or "set a date and time" is sufficient indication to get your secretary moving, then why waste your time launching into

Dear Mr. Jones:

In reply to your letter of 16th inst., I confirm that we shall issue you with our inquiry for...

This is not good language and it's not necessarily courteous. You are wasting your time because "Yes, in July" scribbled on the arriving letter would do the trick. You are wasting your secretary's time (which is your time) in taking your prose down in shorthand and subsequently typing it. All your "ahems" and pauses and phone answerings can stretch a simple letter into ten minutes of your time and twenty minutes of your secretary's. Say what you mean.

Have your secretary, or assistant, whatever term you use

- Do the legwork for data gathering—be it financial or technical—unless it is of great complexity.

- Tot up arriving accounts from various sources so that you get the total picture.

- Give supporting information to help anyone to whom you have addressed a query. By building up confidence, these people will get into the habit of asking the secretary for information instead of asking you.

- Collect routine work, such as a quarterly report you must submit, by chasing up the information and putting it together. All you should have to do is analyze it and comment on it.

The right secretary can be like your "guardian angel." Certainly, my own secretary, Angela, makes me look much more efficient.

The Latest Labor-Saving Toys

Use

- A word processor.

- A tape recorder. If you drive a lot on the job, you will often think out solutions as you travel. To avoid having to recall these or stop the car to jot them down, record as you go.
- Intercom system in the office and/or factory.
- The memory feature on your telephone for those you deal with most often.
- The call-forward feature so your secretary can take your calls when you have a visitor. You can arrange it so that you pick up only if it rings more than two times.
- The call-forward feature in reverse so you don't break your shins trying to answer your secretary's phone when nobody is there.
- Pocket locators for mobile staff—those on a construction site, for example.
- Car phone.
- Computers.

Make sure that everyone reporting to you has secretarial help. Use word processing technology for any item that may need editing or changing or revising. Indeed, straightforward typing must give way to such innovations. Eliminate copy typing if you're still doing this. No checking is then necessary. Use a photocopier for duplicating.

Bypassing the Bottlenecks

Don't allow people in other departments—Personnel, Marketing, Accounting, Finance—to second guess you. If you decide on something, there's always someone somewhere who will try to prove it's a violation of some company policy. What should you do? Give them a week to comment on any matter regarding their area (on a form your secretary will devise and control). This form says "A decision will be made on such and such a day on the enclosed items. If I do not hear from you by this date, I'll assume you have no input." In other words, don't ask them what you can do; tell them what you're doing. This works like magic.

For example, items that used to get gummed up in Personnel for months now come back by hand delivery. Your job is much easier and you don't have to chase around items that have vanished into another department. Your secretary will send off the copy to them and present you with the item for a decision on the date assigned.

You will seldom, if ever, get all the replies to a circular by the deadline you set. It's a bit like rounding up chickens at sundown; it's not always the same chicken that is last. Leave the chicken roundup to your secretary.

Leave a bundle of signed blank sheets with your secretary so that replies to queries can go even when you are out. Sign some of them half way down the page so it looks authentic.

Formicide

Here's an exercise: Put out on a table one copy of every single form used in your area. You may be surprised at some of them. There are the ones you sign hurriedly on Friday evening because they are "wanted at the home office." But you do not study them and are too busy to wonder who uses them.

Other forms routinely run six months behind. How important can they be? Just stop them. One auditor chased such a form, finally tracing it to a wastepaper basket in the sales department of his company. It had been useful once—years ago—and it didn't occur to anyone to discontinue it once it became obsolete.

Stop all traffic in forms through your territory except those directly useful to you. If anyone notices that a form has stopped (a rarity indeed), then demand that a new justification for the form be sent directly to you.

How do you kill useless forms? Try this. Ring your accounts manager; tell her you are off on two weeks vacation and that

- If she kills the forms during the next two weeks, she gets all the credit for rooting out this inefficiency

- If not, you will stop them in three weeks time and defy anyone to get them restarted

The Mail Room Bottleneck

You don't need all correspondence to be routed through a central "registry." Many firms consider it essential to stamp every letter with the date: "Received 26 May 1987." Some even put on the time. This practice is born of the terror among legalists that there will be a court case as to when a letter arrived! The registry is a very busy place with thousands of items coming in and being sorted and distributed. They have the kind of coding system you have just been advised to avoid. It has no relevance to your departments. All incoming mail is delayed by several days and outgoing mail by a day. And for what? It is amusing to be called into a company that has had such a system for many years. When you suggest doing away with it altogether, managers are shocked and say such things as

"How will we get our mail?"

"How can letters find their way to the right place?"

People can't conceive of life without it. The bottom line is that projects are either finished on time or they're not. Holding up correspondence two or three days in a central registry certainly cannot help a schedule.

Internal Communication

Keep a finger on the pulse of your organization. Interview yearly everyone to two steps below yourself. You will then learn such things as

- Who's underutilized
- Which personalities are incompatible
- How bosses are performing
- What you are not doing
- Where junior staff is hurting
- Where responsibilities are unevenly delegated

Have a newsletter run off containing anything that you or anyone else in the company or department thinks everyone should see: large orders placed or landed; competitors' or customers' failures or successes; coming change of office accommodations; interesting discoveries by members of staff.

Produce a house journal (preferably technical, to keep births, deaths, and marriages from taking over) where anyone can write an article under his or her own name. A journal or newsletter could be a vehicle for promoting exposure of and solutions to problems. Find out who has ideas or a knack for something and tell the editor of the journal to worm it out of them for printing. Be careful to get an editor who will keep the journal up to standard and on time, for example, the person who collars you to ask "Why can't we have a good technical newsletter in this place?" Get the better stuff published in outside technical journals.

Don't try to issue the magazine monthly or quarterly. Come out in sequential numbers as the editor gets enough worthwhile information. Three per year for the first year and one or two thereafter should be enough.

Make it the job of all who have information to pass it on. After all, who else knows they have it? We're no longer in the middle ages; no feudal domains.

Stay in Touch

The high-level manager should visit all plants, branch offices, and subsidiary companies at least once yearly. It should never be possible for a complaint to be voiced that you have not set foot on the premises in two years. This will help you get a feel for the real problems, the ones nobody will set to paper because they're dynamite. Watch for the tip of the iceberg.

Don't wait for junior staff or managers to approach you; they may be shy about doing so. Yes, of course, you're the very epitome of kindness, but any person of authority wields a two-edged sword. It makes people antsy, but it's a fact of life.

Send copies of everything coming from the general manager to all your managers—unless the GM says not to. It is better to overtrust your subordinates. If you ever have to apologize for sending them something they shouldn't know about, at least they'll know that they see all they should see.

Besides, the same information is probably already stale news to the custodian and the guys in the mail room, and your managers always know when you are hatching another egg.

Short-circuit the grapevine. Inform your subordinates clearly and regularly about the results of their efforts. If you don't, they'll set up a spy system which will occupy much unnecessary time.

Make it clear to them that if a draft that you sent to them has not been sent back within three days, it is on its way to wherever it should go without their input.

Facilitating Feedback

There is often some friction between sections of an organization; for example, between the design, or "creative," staff and the production, or "technical," staff in an organization. The production people think that nobody consults them when plans are being made for new projects or plant, the execution of which will be up to them. The designers believe that they can get no feedback from the production staff that is of any use in the design function.

In practice, both parties are at fault. To cure the problem, try

- Ensuring that the production people compose operating manuals describing how they operate, including the reasons things are done as they are. Similarly, maintenance instructions and precautions must be documented.
- Ensuring that the design staff read and use all of those operating and maintenance manuals in specifying new equipment, requesting services, etc. In discussions to place orders with a manufacturer, some key operating and maintenance staff should participate in the team led by the designer.

Budgets

Budgets have a life of their own. A good budget is one that is as likely to be overspent as underspent. This concept is very difficult to grasp. A budget that is not realistic is no budget at all. Yet managers at all levels fudge, pad, juggle, manipulate, and massage the figures in order to get what they want or conceal what they don't want known. Weeks are taken arguing about the annual budget allocation, but how much time is given to reviewing the results of last year?

An Oft-Told Tale

For example, it's budget time at Imaginary, Inc.; the managers all come in and present their requirements to the president. She listens in silence and calculates the total. When they are all done, she remarks, "Who do you people think I am, Bob Geldof!" The managers pack their papers and slink out, having seen that the sum of their requests would exceed company income by some 20 percent. They return with figures and plans that are below income, leaving a good profit margin.

Consider an advertising executive in the San Francisco office, who has to submit an annual budget to the boss in New York. What to do? It is known that

- The boss always cuts the submission by 5 to 10 percent.
- Every year there is a new exhortation for "zero-based budgets."
- If a new computer is not included in the budget, he will not be allowed to replace the cranky old one if it finally fails during the year.

So he puts in for a computer plus all the other necessaries and the boss cuts by 7 percent and takes out the computer, responding that the computer will be replaced if and when necessary.

There is a diversity factor at play in budgeting. If ten plants report to

New York and all the budgets are added together, the boss knows from experience that over the past four years the result for the year was 96.2 percent, 95.8 percent, 97.3 percent, and 94.6 percent—even though a flat 5 percent had been cut off each year. He had pleaded that the managers should shoot for a realistic figure, one that each thought would actually occur. Two managers always got it right. But the other eight did not yet really believe that if they ran over budget they would get funds, so they submitted falsely high figures.

The boss should assure all ten that within his overall sum he will switch funds to necessary work late in the year.

Foreseeing the Unforeseeable

Many unforeseen occurrences tend to make expenditure lower than planned; for example

- Cancelled orders
- Staff leaving and not being replaced at once
- Someone dying
- A strike shutting down the plant
- A machine breaking down, with spare parts being paid for next year
- Invoices not arriving on time

We all know that a certain percentage of the work force leaves, retires, or dies each year, but how well do we allow for that? Look at past records for your plant or office to arrive at a good value to allow for this. It is about 3 percent where I work.

Look at the cash flow in the last two months of the year and judge the likelihood of overspending or underspending.

Budgeting need not be a complex, gut-wrenching, mind-boggling process. There should not be a large volume of forms collated in your accounts department for submission to central managers. It is better that each manager send directly to the boss a simple statement on the budget needed for next year, listing

- Performance versus budget for the previous three years
- Changes from last year in orders, personnel, rates of pay, and plant in commission
- Special jobs, recommended in order of performance

To treat the budgeting process as a scientific endeavor by requiring myriad forms to be filled out gives it a false air of importance. More bunkum.

Sidestepping Budgetary Smoke Screens

Budget systems designed by accountants are for control of funds. Thus they will have everything coded by numbers; for example

- Department No. 4
- Activity No. 1224
- Job No. 14

Now some people can decode such numbers without difficulty, but most of us cannot bring ourselves to remember all the numbers and must look them up—every time.

The above information should say something like

- Department: Advertising
- Activity: Copywriting
- Job: The Corpulent Cowboy Project

The wording of budgets is important, too. Why invite unnecessary expenditure by insisting on separate budget control of everything and including on the budget form anticipated expenditures for things like

- Typewriters
- Furniture
- Van purchases

What happens? Each manager looks at the chairs in the office and decides to get a few new ones! It would be better to stop such forms, better to wait until someone thinks to requisition a chair, or until the chair is broken; then get a new one.

Who Says I Can't?

Any notices or circulars forbidding some activity or other are to be viewed with suspicion. You know that where you see the notice No Dumping is where everyone dumps their garbage, because it is an ideal spot away from the public gaze and where there is a huge hole. In Egypt there are signs on all streets forbidding the blowing of car horns. You need ear muffs to block out the deafening din; all cars blow nonstop day and night.

It's the same at work. Putting up a notice will not solve a problem. Indeed, it publicizes the fact that there is a disease. "Please keep this door shut" does not keep the door shut. Why not put an automatic door closer on it and tear up the notice? "Staff shall not spend longer than ten minutes in the employee lounge at morning coffee break" translates roughly as "There is a dreadful abuse here; everyone spends a half hour wasting time in the lounge each morning." Close the lounge and send round coffee trolleys.

The firms with the best code of ethics write nothing. Quite the most elaborate embossed regulation on plagiarism I've seen was issued by an institution that plagiarized work by a colleague and also by myself! They stoutly avoided nailing culprits. The most reputable institutions, the ones that would eject a member for plagiarizing, need no printed rule sheet. Their position is obvious from their past actions.

Information Technology

Do not be led into the trap of thinking that computerization will enable you to make better decisions just because you get

- Faster feed of information
- Neater tables and graphs

No...no.

You've heard the expression "garbage-in garbage-out." The criteria for sound decision making by managers remain subjective and often elusive.

Keeping this in mind, be particular never to let loose a team to custom-tailor software for your firm. Two years later you will be waiting for the result. There are several reasons for such delay:

- A team of computer experts has to be assembled. There will be arguments over what they should be paid and what organizational arrangement is appropriate.
- This team will not be likely to welcome the threat to the gravy train that finishing the task would represent.
- They will try to accommodate every conceivable exigency, getting more and more bright ideas as weeks and months go by.
- The regular staff, to prove to you how much more they know, are likely to raise a spate of objections and throw all proposals back for more changes.

I've seen disastrous, expensive, interminable ventures by such teams.

No, the best and fastest way to introduce computer software is as follows:

- Ask one good performer to locate the best existing package and put it into operation.

- If no existing software fits the bill, challenge one person to produce the goods in two months, or failing that, you will make do with the closest thing available on the market. I've seen the most remarkable successes using this approach.

Updating hardware and software is best done by the users. If you leave a team in control, it will delay its decisions, write reams of unintelligible jargon, and begin to report on its "control" of more and more information facilities.

Speed of information availability or of decision making are not factors in reaching the important decisions in a firm. These are judgmental, based on wisdom, foresight, and experience with whatever graphs and numbers are available as background. The strategic decision depends more on the manager's view of the future, with such unknowns as currency changes and interest rates operative.

"Information" belongs to everyone. It's like brainpower, memory, or thinking. If you attempt to centralize it, you get a section with no responsibility for end results reporting on anything in the firm that requires the use of a computer.

Cardinal Rules of Chapter 2

DO	DON'T
Send all communications from the general manager to all your subordinates	Read anything twice
Have one very shallow drawer that locks for work to be done	Have an in-tray
Keep several pots stirring simultaneously	Have more than one shelf for books
Keep your office tidy	Dictate simple letters
Let your secretary do all reminders and answer all possible letters	Store anything for future reading
Have an informal newsletter	Write submissions containing unanswered queries
Have a formal technical journal	Continue to fill in useless forms
See personally each member of staff at least once annually	Centralize "information"
Have a good filing system	

3

Secrets of Success

Tactics for Change

When you hear anyone say "Why can't we do this?" or "Why doesn't someone do that?" immediately reply, "You do it. How soon can you have something to show?" (unless, of course, undue resources are required). This separates the whiners from the doers. The ones who complain "Nobody tells me anything" or "Nobody lets me do anything" are left behind by the genuine tryers who want to improve things. It is the person who suggests a change who most likely has the conviction to carry it through its frustrations to fruition. Such a grassroots approach to change gets less opposition, because those introducing it are the actual users. It's like gardening. You watch for small, beautiful flowers, then you feed them, shelter them, and encourage them to spread.

Why resent suggestions for change? Sure, it makes your job tougher but you are not here for the easy life.

Don't think that development ceases when you reach your dotage. In fact, it is compounding because it's a cumulative process.

If you get an idea, test it to see if it works. Don't pretend that you came to your idea by way of complex scientific deduction. This sham is what is known as the "scientific method." It is a substitute religion practiced in many seats of learning to justify their existence. Ideas are got by inspiration—Einstein said "I think that theory cannot be fabricated out of the results of observations, but that it can only be invented." Speaking of the search for universal laws, he said "There is no logical path leading to these laws. They can only be reached by intuition, based on something like an intellectual love of the objects of experience."

If you have a novel idea and you are finding it difficult to gain support, use strategy. See if you can get an offer to publish it as an article in a trade magazine. If you get the offer, it confirms that your idea has some validity. Top management will probably have to read your article to give an imprimatur. How better can you get the general manager to read what you have in mind?

An aside: Do not use the words "modern" or "large" when writing any article. It looks a bit ridiculous ten years later when the scale of the thing you were envisioning has been eclipsed by other ideas several times "larger" or more "modern." Yet authors continue to use such categorical words as if all development ceases from today. Remember that manager in 1950 who believed he had the optimum solution to all the company's problems? Guess things didn't quite work out as he'd planned. Of course this can't happen now—we are in a more enlightened age. Right?

Some Scenarios for Change

Two companies that supposedly had been "merged" years later had the same management structure, products, and losses as before. No change. In a merger situation management goes on the defensive, and if you don't act at once, the defenses will be impregnable within a year. You will have been proven too weak to touch them. You are expected to act immediately; not doing so gives hope that you are going to be weak, and this hope will strengthen opposition to change.

On the other hand, why push, push, push until everyone is fed up with you. If you have a good idea that falls on stony ground, wait for the general manager to ask for suggestions in a period of stringency and resurrect it in updated form. Remember, truly creative people never stop with one or two good ideas. They can't win them all. If they score on eight out of ten, they should be pretty satisfied.

If you get caught up in a lifelong crusade with which others don't agree, you'll just get nicknamed after your dog-eared idea. There is a limit to the time and energy worth putting into any one effort to change. The effort to perfect an idea privately can go on intermittently for as long as is necessary. At work though, if no active support forms in three months from launching date, opposition is strong and the change is probably not worth pursuing. If it's a product idea, to test the validity, seek a patent (if it is patentable).

The Naysayers

Introducing major changes from the top—for example, a computerized system for productivity improvement—brings out opposition from the rank-and-file—and even from managers who do not agree with "all this modernization."

To get a major new idea accepted (let's say, for example, you want to introduce a new product line), you have to get your colleagues behind you. How do you do this? You have to get them moving with you:

- Involve them.
- Send drafts of proposals to them for their comments (they will rarely have any serious input; no matter, now they feel part of the scheme).

If you suggest some change or improvement or cost-saving scheme, the following often occurs:

- You get ten reasons why it can't be done. This is a normal reaction from people who should, presumably, have thought of it in the first place.
- Having satisfactorily demolished the first ten objections, you get a very complicated technical explanation as to why it cannot be done. Now you have to learn the technology to see what's being said. Often there is a glaring error in the reasoning—otherwise the defenses need not be so complicated.
- You may believe these arguments and get approval for this more expensive scheme. Then, driving in your car, it strikes you—Gadzooks! Why not do it in a way slightly different from your original idea!
- Now you have just some terminal rumblings as the job is done properly.
- Monday morning quarterbacks, referees in the stands, will abound. They never take part in a game but can shout abuse at you any time you make an apparently wrong move. No one has the right to criticize after the act. If they have anything to say, let it be said at the proper time. You can't stop the complaining, but you are perfectly entitled to tune it out.

Take an example. You get an application to buy two new lathes for a workshop at a cost of $160,000. You query why it is not possible to use the two bought for another shop 200 miles away four years ago that have never been used. What happens?

You are written that the old ones will not fit in the new workshop already built; that to extend the building would cost as much as the new machines; that the old machines will not suit the work to be done at the new factory; that the old machines are so high that cranes cannot lift

equipment over them; the foundations are unsuitable at the new factory; the voltage of the motors does not match, and so on, and so on...
You refute all these by

- Sketching a revised layout putting the lathes at an angle instead of in-line. No building costs are now needed.
- Pointing out that fittings can be bought for $250 that make the old machines suitable for the new factory.
- Pointing out that you can bring all material being lifted around between the lathes. Why go over them?
- Estimating the cost of new foundations at $400.
- Finding new motors that can be purchased for $650.
- Showing that you should not recapitalize the old machines, whereas the new ones would have to be capitalized and attract full overheads (I bet this will not be in the calculations).

And so the fun goes on. Remember that sometimes you will be wrong, but often you will be right, because you are speaking from years of experience—often the sad experience of mistakes you made.

If you ask for a complicated design to be done, pick an excellent designer. You will be told it is not possible. Well, tell her to do it in any case and imply that if she is unable, you will get it done elsewhere. Pride will take over. Magically, the design will emerge, and it will usually be at least good enough that the designer will forget the machinations that were necessary to get her to do it.

Blind Loyalty

Do not be the kind of advocate who sees only one side of the story, chasing facts that fit and using your great powers of persuasion and eloquence.

Why nail your shirt to a mast before you have all the information? You may see it in tatters before the day is out. Shirt nailers lose credibility, even when they have done some homework and think they are perfectly correct. Information that you do not have should be incorporated as soon as it appears. Change your mind when the data shows that you must.

List all the cons as well as the pros for your ideas. This scuttles the opposition as they will have to work to create opposition. If someone is pushing an idea with which you do not agree, list all the arguments that the protagonist put forward (none against will be mentioned), and on the other half of the page list all the reasons against. Do not forget or understate anything in favor. This will allow a fair consideration rather than a one-sided argument.

Take Windmills...Please

Take large windmills as an example. Here are a few of the pertinent arguments. All the "back to the land" people prefer to quote the left column only. High tech advocates favor the other column.

FOR	AGAINST
It's not fair to count the cost of one—make 20,000 and the price will be far lower	Tax rebates on investment made early models appear economic; no tax exemption is now available
They are a free and perpetual source of energy, reducing oil imports	The blades have reversing stresses which eventually break them off, and when one blade breaks, the whole machine is wrecked
The technology is simple compared with a launch to Venus; old technology	The wind blows intermittently, so your investment is idle at least one-third of the year
Look at the wind farms in California; if they can do it, why not us?	There is a law against large windmills: The cost rises very rapidly with height, whereas the power output rises less rapidly. This makes very small ones okay but large ones uneconomic
It does not matter about cost; we must solve the technical problems for the benefit of posterity	If a 2000 kW one in Boone, North Carolina, failed and all the 3000 kW units failed, how can a 4000 kW one work? What happened to the Growian 3000 kW machine in northern Germany? (It never ran, but it looks beautiful!)
If the investment in research and development were one hundredth of that on nuclear energy, of course we would succeed	

Problem-Solving

If there's a problem being discussed, put it right out in the middle of the table for all to see and examine. It's only those who fear superior knowledge or observation who play problems like they were poker. Coolly putting all the cards face up on the table is the hallmark of a winner. There is no time to waste playing the deuce of clubs and waiting to see what the next card will be. Leave playing Snap to the children.

Present the problem correctly in all details the first time. Remember that if you purposely leave one small area uncovered to avoid offending someone or to weight the case in your favor—intending to fix it later—that part of the problem will take center stage. It will grow, and with your blessing.

Get your facts straight. Otherwise you will sway with every breeze. The person who can be persuaded to do anything—provided that the opposition can be kept away—is no better than a tape recorder.

If there are 15 problems and 12 of them have been thrashed out previously, for goodness sake don't reopen any of the 12 again. Some people revel in this. They think it makes their job seem more important. It simply makes them appear confused.

Unless it positively is the right thing to do, don't plug or advocate any line of action that

- Brings more work or power your way
- Is glamorous in its sophistication

For difficult problems such as getting changes in attitudes—say friction and lack of cooperation between your designers and your marketing people—"lean" against the problem. Do not spend all your time trying to get a radical change introduced. By leaning against it your weight is tending to push it along while you are doing all your other work. As soon as some small progress occurs, move after it and lean more. Sometimes you will be surprised how quickly movement occurs. Other times you will be disappointed by how long it takes.

When you are ignorant on a problem, admit at once that you don't know, and ask if anyone present has the answer; 95 percent of the time you'll find that the others will all claim they were just going to pose the same question. They had no such intention.

Managers who are constantly asking for "presentations" from their staff are merely showing that they are unable to understand any written notes on the subject.

When any problem presents itself, for heavens sake look at the simple solutions first. Look at whether someone opened the wrong valve, rather than wandering off theorizing about whether it was a conspiracy by alien visitors from a distant planet. An eminent boiler designer claims that he has yet to find a problem in plant operation that does not have a stupidly simple explanation.

In problem-solving, the judgment of business risk or technical risk cannot be reduced to mathematics. Accountants dearly wish that this were so. An illusion of science is given by so-called "risk-analysis." But a simple piece of equipment can cause a huge disaster, whereas very exotic equipment may not do so.

It is the judgment and the experience of the individual that matters. Pretending that a formal reliable judgment of risk can be done by filling in a "risk" form to be run through a computer is nonsense. The responsibility for taking the risk must rest on the shoulders of the manager in charge of bidding for and doing the job.

Clear Vision, Straight Action

Remember, you can't win them all. An irate customer once told a manager that the speed of his satisfactory reply was proof that the company was rotten from top to bottom.

Know the game you are in; stay in step. Go back to college if you have to, or study to be on top of the job. Otherwise you will be—not just appear to be—more and more of a bluffer. I call this "presbyopia" in management (presbyopia = sight of an old man).

Don't make excuses:

"My report is not as exhaustive and complete as I would have liked..."(Quite the longest report I ever read was introduced like that.)

"Annual leave and pressure of work prevented us from..."

Never allow yourself to believe that decisions you have to make are tougher than anyone else's. It's not the decisions that are more difficult; you're making them that way. Everyone's decisions, if we are all in the right jobs, are equally easy, from the window cleaner's to the general manager's.

Never be deflected off the job at hand. If the task is to travel the shortest route between Boston and Denver, don't stop off looking at cow palaces on the way. If you find yourself doing this, it's a sure sign you don't like the task. And what does that mean?

Going off on other tasks that are not appointed and not relevant is a common disease. Could it be fear of tackling the job you have been given? "Ah," you say, "I'm just clearing the ground to get at the job." But look, you cannot be called to account for failure to excel in your diversions, and you cannot be seen to fail in your main task because you have not begun it yet.

Avoid opening up problems any more than necessary with additional considerations such as

"What of the influence of x?"

"Should we consider y and z?"

"Possibly p, q, and r should be investigated?"

Here's a mentality hellbent on turning 1 problem into 20. It is studded with "might," "maybe," "possibly"—not the facts and figures prepared in advance that will help bring about a decision.
Don't look for difficulties:

"What would Thurmond think if I did this?"

"I'd better chat this over with Charlotte."

Aren't things difficult enough as it is? You're just looking for an excuse to avoid making a decision.
Don't believe a sales rep's glowing forecasts of future business either. Sales reps are paid to be optimists. Go for cold-blooded market-research, statistical-analysis forecasts.
Finally, don't expect grand improvements in a week. Rome wasn't built... Go for the steady, regular improvements.

Initiative

Initiate something every week. What else are you there for? If you don't initiate and instigate, you are a constriction in the flow of work and decisions. By initiate, I mean start something which will result in improvement and work it out to a useful stage. I do not mean you should sit there firing off salvos:

"Why don't they standardize the procedure for...?"

"What about if we introduce a new line of...?"

No management job should contain less than 25 percent initiation and instigation, and the more senior the post, the higher should be the percentage.
Try having a day or part of a day in which you have no appointments. Then you can get down to planning improvements that you consider worthwhile. After all, if you don't improve things, you are hardly needed. Things would surely go along in their same old way without you.
Do your work! Do *your* work! Do not go around seeking out someone to do it for you. The boss will know; colleagues will get irritated with this drone that picks all their brains and puts the results down over his signature. If this is the case, you can be sure they'll get together even-

tually and impose an embargo on information, just to see if this cuckoo can do anything besides manipulate other people's abilities.

Have you ever been behind a driver who seemed to *want* the next traffic light to go red? Some managers act the same way. They delay and ponder and look around, hoping so hard that something will stop the problem or make it manageable that they stop doing anything.

It is a good thing to learn by asking those in your company who have experience. But that is different from intellectual laziness, which leads you to avoid tackling any problem.

Each person should try to effect economies worth 10 percent of the turnover of his section of the firm—every year.

Containing Your Job

Confine yourself to those tasks that cannot progress while you are on holiday or sick. If all goes fine when you are golfing, why come back to redo, comment, undo, or, as others see it, mess up or slow up? This includes signing documents and forms that need to be approved by a person of your status. They'll get signed in your absence.

Once in a while, formally ask your direct subordinates to pen you a note saying what work they think you should delegate completely to them. Then do it. Do not try to get your equals to do likewise. They will not until their subordinates complain that they have less delegation than elsewhere.

If there is someone among your subordinates who knows more than you do on any given question or issue, bring that "expert" along to any meeting on the subject. If you don't, it'll look like you're trying to be seen as the expert in this discipline. You may end up looking inept instead. And your subordinates will either be pacing the floor or giggling it up.

Whenever possible, refer your boss to one of your subordinates who knows the answer to a problem. NEVER, NEVER, NEVER act as a go-between, getting the answer and relaying it.

And don't become a glorified public relations officer for your company:

- Attending official openings of new office blocks
- Bear-leading visitors
- Inspecting the plant as an interested amateur
- Receiving representatives hawking equipment of marginal interest to staff three steps lower in the organization
- Going to luncheons in the local Ritz every day and cocktail parties every evening

- Attending funerals

Keep Your Eye on the Ball

You must know the business you are in—in detail. Otherwise, when you visit one of your other facilities, everyone will figure it's a "showing the flag" exercise. You will never notice that six drain pumps are out of order or that ten sootblowers are inoperable. If your plants have to have these things, then you must know all about them. When you arrive and walk around the plant floor with the line supervisor, you must be in a position to ask why they are out of order—and know enough not to be put off by stupid excuses that are not true.

Don't let yourself believe you have a full-time job "supervising" a dozen persons' work. They should be well able to get on without supervision. You thought you could before you got your last promotion, didn't you? Never do anything that can be done better, equally well, or nearly as well by a subordinate.

Ask your direct subordinates and the next level below them what major improvements could be made in your operation. Get, say, 25 suggestions, put them in rough order of value, and tackle them. Get at least 20 done in a year. Name who is to do each—and give yourself a fair share, the ones which can't reasonably be done by anyone else. Review them each quarter to see whether any should be dropped owing to changing circumstances. If you get stuck at No. 2, don't stop or slow down. Let it simmer and carry on down the list.

Never deal during working hours with matters connected with outside activities:

- Professional association work
- Golf club committee work

You may argue that this is useful to your company, increasing your influence and sources of information, but there are extreme cases of managers who do little else. The disease reaches epidemic proportions among more senior managers, junior managers coming to believe that their seniors do little else but phone each other on committee matters.

What is the main task you should be doing? It is not

- Watching others work
- Checking others' work
- Advising others
- Reprimanding or cajoling others

Those should be only a small portion of your job.

You should concentrate on where there is poor performance and money being lost. And you must improve ways of doing things; that is, you, personally, must innovate. Most people shy away from all these main tasks because they are so busy with the trivia. Concentrate on the "Pareto few" —i.e., the 20 percent of things which will make the biggest difference to performance in the coming years.

Responsibility vs. Accountability

Don't show your ignorance by declaring that you do not see the difference between delegating responsibility and delegating accountability. It's simple.

If you do a good job, the credit is taken by everyone above you on the ladder, right up to the president. After all, that's why you were picked to do the job, so that your boss could take a large slice of the credit. But if you screw up a job, you and you alone are clearly to blame. This is delegation at its best. You understand now, don't you? No? We'll come back to it later.

Sales

One cannot be knowledgeable about everything. I must confess that in the marketing and sales aspects of business, I am mainly familiar with the heavy engineering business, which is very different from retail sales, department stores, or selling sheep. My thoughts and ideas, then, are influenced by this fact.

Sales is the one field that is an exception to the rule "good at one job, good at another." Pessimists must be kept away from sales, no matter how good they are in another job. Don't make the mistake of promoting someone into sales because she "is in line for promotion and there is nothing else going that suits her talents."

Sales Organization and the Sales Rep

The organization of a sales department is unimportant. What is important is to have there the one or two persons gifted in selling. You know what I mean—think of some of them—those who went single-handed to

China or Saudi Arabia and came back with huge remunerative contracts.

Successful salespeople are usually self starters, know what they can and cannot do, and act like the general manager. They believe they can sell to their own management any deal they strike with a customer. They don't delegate; they work out of suitcases; they love travel; they are gregarious, with endless funny stories (and can thus be boring if you are in a hurry); they are well liked by people of all cultures and creeds. They also know their own limitations and are smart enough to select the best people in their organization when expert technical, financial, or legal advice may be required.

A long time ago, when Ralph Cordiner was chairman of General Electric, he wrote in one of his Cordiner Reports that for years he thought the reason a customer would buy from G.E. rather than other competitors was because the G.E. product was technically superior. He was told this every day by his engineers. After a number of years, he came to the conclusion that although G.E. product was excellent, the competitors' products also worked well, and that G.E. was most successful with those customers among whom the G.E. salesperson had established good relations over a number of years and was well liked. In those cases where the competitor's salesperson was closer to and better liked by the customer, G.E. was mostly unsuccessful in obtaining orders. In those cases where the G.E. salesperson was actually disliked, independently of any competition, they never sold anything.

If a sales office grows, and grows more bureaucratic, adding all sorts of people doing calculations, desk studies, computer studies, writing circulars to control traveling expenses, querying why Travali spent two days in Ireland, and so forth, the message that comes across is "Since we don't know how to get business here, in the meantime we are cutting back on overheads."

But why not do away with the most conspicuous overheads—these extra people?

Such a group will tend to do things that look as if they might yield dividends in new business, for example, opening extra offices and putting more staff there, or paying dollars to foreign agents with poor performance records. You should look at actual results.

Getting Business

Getting a very large chunk of business is usually achieved by a senior person in the organization. Take a look at the large manufacturing companies or consultancy firms. It is the partners or their equivalents who go out and get business such as

- Petrochemical factories
- Power stations
- Jet aircraft

The person who gets business is the one who knows the full scope of the business, can answer all queries and make decisions on the spot, can satisfy the buying company with superior ideas and economics, and will sign on behalf of your firm there and then.

The actual detailed design and construction is done by the total organization, but no large piece of business is got, or is ever likely to be got, by an assistant production engineer in your factory—even if you let him off to try!

If you are the buyer, who do you expect to call looking for an order worth $1,000,000? In practice, you get the following:

- The chief engineer from a Swiss or German company, with two or three sidekicks
- The sales manager (privately educated, you see) from some English firm, with a small team from technical areas
- The vice president or president from a U.S. firm, with two or three underlings (they will probably bring a lawyer who will object to 50 clauses in your specifications)
- Fifteen or twenty Japanese with all sorts of titles

I've had the experience of wanting to buy from a particular firm, and they were reluctant to bid. I had to ring up a top director to force them to bid. They assumed we would not buy for "political reasons." Never, never, cut off a market with such pessimistic assumptions. We placed an order for $15,000,000 against the opposition of the sales force responsible for making the sale!

Don't be negative when trying to get business. Whining, questioning inquiries turn prospective buyers away. Leave your lawyers at home. If you want to do business in any country besides your own, then you must do it their way. Let your lawyers advise you privately.

If a prospective buyer asks if you will bid for a project, say yes. Do not ask for the answers to 14 questions before you make up your mind. Who says you are going to get the job? All you're being asked is if you want it. Dealing with a buyer is not the same as arguing with your finance department. All your queries can be ironed out as the details of your hoped-for contract are worked out.

It's like playing a round of golf on a new course. There's the kind of player who just hits the ball up the middle of the first fairway. Then there's the one who worries about out-of-bounds that are recorded on the card for the 3rd and 5th holes, or the lateral water hazard at the 2nd.

A good salesperson is somewhat like the goose that lays golden eggs. The gift cannot be stolen or copied easily. Getting lectures from a good salesperson will not make you equally excellent.

It is important for a salesperson to develop a good personal relationship with the customer. The best of them seem to understand what is on the customers' minds, which is not always what comes out of their mouths. You can tell when someone close to you is not in agreement with you—by tone of voice, hesitation, whatever. So it must be in the customer relationship.

Too Busy for Business

Many people in business are so confused and preoccupied that they are "too busy for business."

Look at the post office clerk when you want to buy some stamps. She may be filling in some forms, or counting stamps, or closing the hatch, but is not available to sell stamps immediately.

Go into a store and try to buy something. All the assistants who are so annoyingly solicitous before you decide on something seem to disappear behind clothes racks when you're ready to check out.

Look into the ticket office at a train station. You have 30 seconds to catch the train. Where is the clerk? Certainly not waiting to sell you a ticket—probably ringing up to order more tickets, or tidying up heaps of forms—but adamantly preoccupied, with his back to you.

Try getting served in a restaurant. The waiters are busy clearing off other tables, or folding napkins in a corner.

All this activity gives the worker the illusion of being very busy all day. There is hardly time to do the required tasks. Parkinson's Law—the expansion of peripheral secondary activities to the extent that they almost squeeze out the key task—really applies in these instances. If the key task was the only one considered, then the job would appear unimportant and the person would consider that the job was not keeping him busy. This is not acceptable. Pride is hurt. So the natural reaction is to completely occupy the hours of the day and rationalize it. Wait a minute... Back up. What business are you supposed to be doing? Well, do it.

Consider any occasion when you suddenly moved into a truly busy job. You look back and wonder how on earth you spent the day in your previous post.

The logical conclusion from all this is that you are not 100 percent busy in your job. You fill in the day doing peripheral things that are easy to do and allow you to daydream as you do them. Leave the peripheral activities until there is spare time, with no customers present, to do these ancillary things.

There is nothing wrong with having bursts of activity interspersed with periods of easy activity. If you try to keep at fever pitch all day, every day, you will not succeed because you will not have sufficient energy to sustain such a pace.

It is in the regulation of the periods of easier activity that success lies. Fit them in when you are not disaccommodating a customer or colleague by doing so.

Judgments and Decisions

"Making decisions" is not simply "choosing a course of action." Ask the custodian to choose whether you should or should not buy a new computer. You'll get an answer. The custodian can say "yes" or "no" and thus "decide." This, however, is better known as a guess.

The object of the game is to PASS WISE JUDGMENTS. To do this you must hear the evidence of the protagonists. You must have set down before you all the problems associated with a YES judgment and all the problems associated with a NO judgment. If you get a submission from the computer division recommending the purchase of new equipment, with a long list of fantastic advantages, smell a rat. No single product has all those advantages over the competition or it would be the only one in use. Nor is any single product exclusively advantageous, without drawbacks. What of the initial extra cost, the greater expense of software or other supporting materials, the dearth of canned programs for a certain aspect of your business?

Any fool can make an arbitrary decision. But who, besides Solomon, of course, do you know who can display truly good judgment?

An arbitrary decision does not finish the matter. Your subordinates will be back with further efforts to force you to a wise judgment. Do not think that because you penned your signature to 25 decisions this week, you are proving your worth. Agreeing to accept the cheapest evaluated tender, appoint the candidate selected by the interview board, or pay the rate accepted in the industry, doesn't count as decision making, let alone exercising judgment. It's either automatically applying a preestablished set of standards or simply rubberstamping someone else's decision.

Of all the things submitted to you, if you decide No to

- 20 percent—Either you have a selection of idiots reporting to you or you are one yourself and don't know what's going on.

- 5 percent—You are asserting the veto to prove your presence.

- 1 percent—This is tolerable in a rapidly changing environment and if the No calls for additions or alterations before approval.

- 0.1 percent—This is about normal; the No should normally be on something left open, pending a Yes or No decision.

- 0.0 percent—You are a rubber stamp.

Remember, many decisions that company rules stipulate must have your signature can be signed by someone else in your absence. I've known submissions held back for months until a certain manager—"the veto lady"—was on vacation.

Set rules for what is to be inspected abroad, for example, or how often contract meetings are to be held in Australia on a main contract. Thus one approval is all that is needed, instead of approving each separate visit. Also, set rules for the assessment of bids so that you can check them more quickly.

When dealing with outside agencies with a regulatory say in what you do, the following tips may be helpful. Never resort to any outside agency, especially the government, for a decision or direction as to what you should do. You will, most likely, get no answer, in which case you're back where you started. If you get any input at all, it will either be

- Negative, which will stop you from doing what *you* should do.

- A half-dozen points needing clarification. This will only delay the job, and in answering the six queries, you will likely generate 36 more, and so it goes.

You will be unlikely to get a direction because now someone in that outside body has to take responsibility, and he may be reluctant to accept it.

Instead, you should write telling the outside agency that you now propose to act as follows. Say what you plan to do and when you will do it. Usually silence will follow, which you can assume "means consent." No negative response is likely because the outside agency would now be assuming the responsibility of stopping you, and this they will be very loath to do.

So to get on with your job, assume responsibility and do not try to pass the decision outside your organization.

The Litigation Cop-Out

If a difference of opinion arises with another firm, don't avoid your responsibilities by going to court to settle the issue. Negotiate and settle the affair. You must be a chess player in this situation, judging the cost gap between you and your counterpart in the other organization versus the cost of litigation. If you want to say "the court decided," you avoid criticism from at least one angle because you are deferring to a body which is supposed to have more wisdom. But you have abrogated your responsibility and you are not doing your job, especially if the cost of the court case would be more than the difference between the parties.

Civil servants like to let matters go to court:

- Nobody can accuse them of being soft and giving a contractor too much money.

- The court's decision is the law of the land and their job is to apply the law of the land—no matter that a settlement for $200,000 could have been effected rather than $1,000,000 of legal fees and a $500,000 judgment to be paid to the contractor.

Who wins? The legal profession.

A court case is occasionally unavoidable, but it should not exceed one every 10 years or so. Some say that the United States is litigation mad. In other countries litigation is quite rare.

What to Avoid in Decision Making

Delaying a decision doesn't make it easier. Two conflicting views are with you for a decision—get on with it. If you wait until the last possible day, you will be under pressure and will appear to have panicked. Such delaying is often done in the hope that protagonists will finally agree without bothering you. Nonsense! Often they know what should be done, but it will remove a degree of power from one of them. Sometimes they have agreed privately to the outcome, and you're in trouble if you rule the opposite way.

Sometimes two conflicting views arise, and you are called on for a "decision." If the two parties should cooperate, write on top "I'm not King Solomon. Work this out between you by Thursday and write and let me know what you did in the best interest of this firm." You know and they know what should be done—but make *them* do it. Otherwise, you'll keep getting such submissions.

Delaying decisions is not going to save the firm money. If you hold up a $120,000 decision for a month, do you save the interest on the value (about $1000)? No. The manager involved will have you sized up and will build a month's allowance into the time schedule. You are wasting everyone's time. If your subordinates have a bring forward file for your activities, it is a very serious reflection on your efficiency.

Don't invent "principles" to suit some ad hoc decision. A principle never/always to take a certain line means that there is no reason whatever to justify it, that you just like the cut of it.

Don't be disgruntled if all the facts are presented to you on a plate and you have no comment to add. Agree on the spot. Don't feel superfluous.

Never make an arbitrary decision to put someone in his place. This is army tactics and you are not in the army. No one of worth will ever be put in his place!

It is no excuse for delaying decisions that

- You were in Germany all the week; were you sleeping at the airports and on the planes?

- All your assistants were down with flu; everyone is capable of twice the output normally achieved, so get on your bicycle.

Don't get scared and suggest

- Appointing a consultant
- Setting up a committee (see Chapter 1)
- Leaving it until the next meeting

The Procrastinator

There is rarely an appropriate time to decide anything. The decision will not be easier a month down the road. You may have more information but some is likely to be for and some against the lines of action already established.

"If we wait until Christmas, we will have another six months experience."

"I'm new in this place, so I'd better wait a year or so until I know what is going on."

"I'll send it to Personnel for their opinion; otherwise I might get into trouble for breaking regulations."

"I'll post it to Mary Lou—maybe she is better positioned to decide this one."

"When we get a strategy, and following that a business plan, we can see exactly where we should be aiming."

This person is like an eight-way intersection with signs pointing all directions. There is no destination for anything.

For many people the last inch is the hardest to complete. If this trait shows up in a young person, danger bells should ring. If not cured quickly, the disease becomes ingrained and can't be rooted out. You may see someone doing a report who can't finish it. They have a bulky briefcase that they carry from home to work and back. It is hard to understand why they can't just complete it and get on to something else. Such a person will be almost useless at work.

Have you ever heard this: "Decisions nowadays are tougher than previously?" Some people are convinced that managers 20 years ago had an easy time. They did not have to deal with computers or television or airplanes. They used slide rules and had to travel on trains. The speed of calculating and travel are being confused with the difficulty of decisions. It is as if Hannibal had an easy time because he used elephants to cross the Alps into Italy; or as if Julius Caesar had it easy because he had no telephones, automobiles, airplanes, computers, or electricity, and used an abacus to calculate (how did he multiply XVIII by MCCCV?). Do you think it was easy to conquer and control western Europe 2000 years ago!

Decisions are just as easy or hard as they ever were or ever will be in the future. So get on with it without moaning.

Platitudes

Expressing a vague desire for improvement helps no one:

"Overtime should be cut."

"We have too many staff here."

"People must tighten their belts."

"A positive attitude is needed."

It's your job to do all these things. The abstract is not helping! Such platitudes often emerge from personnel and accountancy groups.

"Years of experience has shown..." is a euphemism for "Let's rest on our laurels." It tries to stop reasonable criticism or suggestion for improvement. It says "How dare you have the impertinence to query our procedures."

Planning

Many people are frightened by the word "plan." They say "I'd be no good at planning; I just like production or operations..." But there is no mystery to planning. Indeed, in all jobs good planning is the secret to success. You plan out

- What you are going to do this morning
- All jobs that must be done in the next week and their priorities

What is meant by the "Planning Department" is that it is the place where plans are laid for

- Changes in technology
- New factories
- New products (be it shoes or airplanes)

Each firm has to plan ahead or it will gradually fizzle out.

The length of time considered for planning purposes is determined by how long it will take to effect the change; for example

- A nuclear power station takes about eight years from beginning the plan to completion.
- Building a new cement factory takes about three years.
- Developing a shortcut in the production of an existing drug would probably take between six and nine months.

So each industry must be planning ahead by the length of time it takes to do whatever is being considered.

Each section of a diversified business must do its own planning. Having got plans from all sections of the firm, an overall plan can be drawn up for a whole company, ensuring that no duplication of work occurs and that nothing is forgotten. There is a genuine danger that the different sections in a firm will be attacking a problem without the knowledge that the other is also trying to find a solution. Thus an overall plan tying the individual plans together is necessary.

Planning criteria are important. By changing a word or number you can radically affect the results. As an example, if you say that once in five years on average you are allowed to fail to meet the required load, you get one result; but if you are allowed to fail once per month, then you get a cheaper solution. So devote careful consideration to each and every so-called sacrosanct criterion which forms the basis of the plan.

It is a good idea to have planning done as follows. Have a group of people to draw up a plan using all the best techniques available. Since that group may have a bias, or may miss something, have a group of experienced persons to review the plan. In practice, this is useful to:

- Prevent a plan that advocates something off-the-wall, like meeting the energy needs of the entire United States with wave power.
- Prevent a plan that is biased in favor of one solution to the exclusion of others.
- Ensure that no unusual or novel solution is missed.

The "overseers" should be very experienced and should represent a cross section of the firm—design, operation, finance, and planning—and should include the boss to whom it will be recommended (the latter as chairperson).

This process may be looked upon by the section that draws up the plan as an insult, but what you want is the correct solution. This scheme works well. When the "expert" group has eventually given an imprimatur, then the plan is recommended to the boss, who then has the final look at it all.

This type of plan is then incorporated into the overall company plan and presented to the president of the company. The final judgment of what to recommend to the board must rest with the president. This is one of the main functions of that job—"What should the firm do over the next 5 to 10 years?" No amount of computer studies will help—the judgment has to be made by wisdom.

The Company Mission

Some companies spend much time getting the "company objectives" set down. It all sounds sensible. How can a company operate successfully without any aim? If there is no common objective, the various divisions could be pulling in opposite directions.

But look at the generalized platitude that sometimes emerges. It can't be long, so it can't say much, and it must not be too specific because it is a "corporate long-term objective," so it looks something like

To provide an acceptable product to the customers at optimum cost

with the words "acceptable" and "optimum" totally vague and unmeasurable.

Check it out—nobody subsequently reports program against such a statement because that is just not possible.

Setting an overall objective before building up the economics and steps to achieve that objective is merely wishful thinking. For example, suppose a firm sets an objective to increase market share by 15 percent over four years.

This may put the firm into liquidation or make it more successful. This extra 15 percent may not be remunerative. Indeed, reducing market share may be more economic. Plans showing good sales are easily written. They can justify investment proposals, but a close look at such forecasts is always needed. So find out; get facts and figures.

Writing large policy documents is a useless exercise. Consider a personnel department that issues an annual plan. It will be full of platitudes.

- Policy will be flexible and adaptable.

- Contingency planning should be considered.

- A structured approach to staff development will be a priority.

- A positive approach to the management of people will be fostered.

It will speak of better planning for the future. It implies that there will be less ad hoc reaction to future events. Any such document will assert that it is not a vague wish but a practical plan. The more the protestation, the more useless and impractical the document.

Long-Term Planning

Long-term planning is planning for a time span beyond the time taken to build any necessary new facilities, factories, plants, or to launch any new drug or computer product. It is thus planning for what's at the end of the rainbow. Before setting off on a long-term plan, look at the long-term plans of the whole country and have a laugh.

Long-term planning is great fun. It is best done when you are planning to do nothing. At such a time you can develop wonderful plans; for example, your program could read something like this:

Policies Process	Framework
Objectives	Reference Plan
Growth Potential	Corporate Strategy
Strategic Gap	Goals
Position Matrix	Strategic Objectives
Planning Assumptions	Strategies
Alternatives	Mission Statement
Organizational Relationships	Operating Plans
General Thrust	Specific Criteria

The order of these headings is unimportant.

Getting this far will take about two years. By that time all the original assumptions on raw materials costs, energy costs, and market prices will be out of date, so you will have to start all over again. But the next set of plans will be done by a different team that will blissfully ignore their predecessor's efforts.

If there is a need to do something, the planning process is entirely different. It will all happen quickly with an absence of voluminous reports. Facts and figures will be studied and decisions made on the best available information.

You can hardly admit that you have no long-term plan. You could be criticized because:

- If you have no long-term plan how do you know where you are going?

- How can all groups go in the same direction without one overall long-term plan?

Companies with long-term plans are usually those with money to burn.

High-Level Corporate Documents

Documents on what is termed "policy" will be prepared for discussions by the board. Such documents have little to do with the ongoing work being done or to be done. They will be on topics thought up by management as suitable to fill up the agenda for the next board meeting.

With a set date for the next board meeting, a mad rush ensues to have a report done. The report must look well: glossy cover, fine-colored diagrams, flowing language.

Because the report is about something that is not being done, most of the board members will not read it. They will just scan the synopsis that should be in the front.

So, much of the time of senior staff will be occupied writing and fine-tuning such reports. Maybe it is a necessary evil. It keeps board members busy. It is an insulation layer between the board and the company.

The board has one key function: the appointment—or the removal—of the president. It can even have a say in the selection of vice presidents. But apart from that, it should let the company operate with a minimum of interference.

The reason the board should not interfere is simple. The president must use judgment in deciding what is to be done to improve efficiency or to gain markets. So an insulation layer must exist to prevent the board from also trying to exert its judgment of such topics on the organization. And the judgment of a group of ten will be disjointed, a compromise, not courageous, and somewhat disinterested.

Cardinal rules of Chapter 3

DO	DON'T
Instigate something every day	Waste more than three months on any idea unless you have considerable support
Let the instigators of ideas have their head	Leave problems to fester
Confine yourself to what can only be done by you	Delay decisions
Put your cards face up on the table	Make excuses
Get all your facts right first time	Stray from the target
Have at hand records of your job	Open up a problem beyond the least possible
Budget well	Become a glorified public relations officer
Set main objectives for your group	Make arbitrary decisions
Be composed	Have ad hoc unlinked plans
Keep your planning simple	Occupy your time on peripheral activities
Intervene when a program is running late	Overdo long-term planning
Concentrate on the core of your job	

4

Project Management

Much of what we do in our work could be termed "project management." What this means is that something is being done which

- Must be on time
- Must be within budget
- Must perform excellently when completed

It is not routine work; it involves some innovation. Many people are
very good at one of the three items listed above; some are good at two.
But it is no use

- Having it done on time and to budget if it never operates properly
- Having a wonderful performance which was on time but cost several
  times its budget

What you have to do is get all three right, with no excuses.

Look Before You Leap

A project can be

- Installing a computer system
- Publishing a book
- Launching a new factory or product
- Extending the office block
- Opening a restaurant
- Laying a path from the sidewalk to your front door

Planning a project should include a "what if" session; for example, what if the market grows at a different rate from that predicted? What if political instability occurs in a neighboring state? Or what if you have a very bad spell of weather? A what-if session will lead to certain protective actions to insulate the project against disaster. If a project consists of four identical units to be constructed, then the protection could be

- Cancellation clauses in the contracts for units 3 and 4

- Agreed fees, negotiated at the contract placing stage, to be added per year of delay of units 2, 3, or 4

Once the project is under way, it's too late to get the supplier to agree to this.

These are not just theoretical possibilities. In fact, two neighboring states were constructing identical four-unit projects. One state's contract contained the above clauses, the second's did not. The result was that

- The state with no clauses covering delay or cancellation ended up with one unit built that it did not need—a costly exercise.

- The other state delayed the third unit by two years and cancelled the fourth to match precisely its market growth.

On Time

Be realistic. If you are building a new office complex, you know that something will go wrong during the project. A storm may blow down your largest construction crane; a strike may occur; some materials may be faulty and have to be replaced. So in a program of four years, allow two months for "acts of divine intervention" or strikes. Write that on all editions of the program and aim to complete the project in three years and ten months.

Well and good if you finish earlier than the four, but the chances are you will just succeed. Also, acknowledging the possibility of strikes on the program will be a deterrent to anyone thinking of going on strike hastily because it can be seen that a two-month strike can be accepted without delaying the program.

Have the program for each aspect of a project made by people who have done it before—successfully.

Make sure that any critical item—materials or parts—is made early enough. Have a "what can delay this project" session right at the start and work out how to avoid possible disasters. Allow a margin for error so you can avoid situations in which you have to sacrifice either your schedule or the quality of the work.

Have the minimum critical path analysis necessary and send smaller and smaller reports as you report up the line—one page to the department head. Report only by exception, showing what is late against program at present.

Lose Patience

When should you lower the boom? Don't wait too long. For example, if someone is trying to put equipment into commission and is a month longer than scheduled without success, do not believe anyone who says

- He is just having bad luck. Look at his CV; he has great experience.
- The computer bugs are all out now.
- Tomorrow it will be okay.
- Your check's in the mail.

Do not leave a manager on any section of a project where work is falling behind schedule or not being properly done. This is particularly true on a project spanning several years. If the project takes only two months, by the time you could get a replacement the job would be finished. So you had better just lend a hand. But you can't do that for three years, so act fast and change now.

Do not wait. Move in today. Supplant the person in charge of this work. Whenever you replace an incompetent person, the replacement you get must be startlingly better than the other. The difference must be obvious from the moment the new one arrives. You will not regret having moved. Indeed, you may regret waiting so long.

Cost Control—Keep It Simple

If you are selling something, do not work out the cost of producing it, add a profit margin, and then go out and try to get that price.

No, keep it simple:

- Look and see at what price that thing is selling, be it a steam turbine or a tube of toothpaste.
- Take that price and decide if you can make it, with a profit margin, for that price.

- If not, then examine whether better and cheaper ways can be devised to meet this target.

- If other companies can do it, why can't you? Reexamine the situation to see where you are failing and fix those failings.

The costs and overheads in companies tend to rise and fall to absorb the sales price that can be got for products. In good times, everyone gets a new desk and automobile; in bad times, no extravagances are allowed. The shareholders are largely insulated from seeing the swings in margins achieved.

The same approach applies to estimating the cost of doing something. Do not allow anyone to estimate the cost of building something by compiling a thousand sheets full of such items as

- 3-inch pipe, 200-feet long: $200

- Four steel doors: $600

- One crane: $26,000

This is a useless approach when each of the prices is tentative (and probably on the high side) because the compiler will be held responsible for the estimates.

No. You start at the other end with macro estimates; for example, dollars per kilowatt for such a plant built in New Jersey, completed in the year 1982. This should match what is being achieved elsewhere. If your performance has not matched others previously, then stop here and find out why. Do you need better construction equipment? Also, allow for peculiarities of your plant. Does it need a jetty out to sea?

When you have solved that stage, then work out the cost for each major item of the plant (for example, turbines, boilers, controls) and for each auxiliary system and break down how many dollars are available for each of these.

That is all the money that is to be made available and you have to work to that. It is perfectly ridiculous to work out the price of some minor items (like doors) for a $72,000,000 job. A $15 difference in the cost of doors is not going to change the end result. The accuracy of the overall estimate is about plus or minus 2 percent, and a contingency sum of that amount is to be included in the total sum.

Have graphical sheets showing how expenditure is going against budget, and, naturally, the payments made compared to actual work done. This is difficult for some work—like civil engineering foundations—but try to get an accurate scheme.

Pitfalls

You must watch carefully proposals for project investments from a group that is short of work. Such groups will want to do anything and will rationalize the necessity to go ahead with some pet scheme. Look at the assumptions, because all the conclusions follow automatically from the assumptions. Do not get lost in the logic of getting from the assumptions to the conclusions. If you do, you have already conceded that the project is viable and wise. Indeed, the finer the cover and colored diagrams, the greater the danger that the project is not viable, and that a key assumption is wrong.

Big Is Not Beautiful

You do not have to try to make the largest, highest, most electrifying project. To reduce this to the point of absurdity, if you try to make an airplane that carries 60,000 passengers, (a) it will be too expensive, and (b) it won't fly.

Reliability frequently goes down as size goes up, once you pass a certain size for equipment. Many dispute this, but look at the statistics for power stations, for example. The figures are published in the United States. They show that the breakdown of ordinary conventional plant rises inexorably as the unit sizes go from 300 megawatt up to 1000 megawatt.

You must take this principle into account when planning a project. Do not try to fool yourself, your customers, or your shareholders by pretending that you will do better than everyone else. Granted, there are exceptions to every rule—someone will point to a unit in California that is doing better. But check carefully:

- How often is it started and stopped?
- How is it fueled? Maybe it is a particularly easy fuel to use.

Projects of dubious economics are often the ones with the most impressive brochures—good thing; they need them!

Resources

Availability of help to do a job depends on only one thing: whether the supervisor who has the spare people wants to release them.

If you want to pull together a team from within your company to take on a new project, you will find that

- Because other managers did not land the project, they will tend to be uncooperative in lending you people or resources, "We are down four on our necessary staff here already."
- You will get staff from managers who know you personally. They will give you one or two and then have to scout around for people to fill the gaps.
- If staff are released by a manager who does not know you, that is a remarkable person.

If, on the other hand, you are the person doing the recommending and you give away a dud with a glowing recommendation, no other supervisor will trust you again. Then, even your good swans will not get to fly. Good staff will come to view your area as a graveyard for ambitions and you will reap a harvest of stumors.

Here's another tricky, resource-related situation. A branch company wants you to invest $10,000,000 in a new development. The technology and process is new and you have grave doubts about the output (which is heavily weather dependent) because you checked on actual outputs obtained in another country. They were only half the advertised figures. A simple solution that the president of a New Jersey company applied is this. He said, "Okay, go ahead, provided the manufacturer of the new technology invests 50 percent." They did not and the project died.

Performance Ratios

Do not pay too much attention to the debt-to-equity ratio of your company. The sense of this is seen by the following:

- If you have a product that is excellent, is well made, is priced to match the world's best, and if you have an efficient, dynamic, innovative work force, then it matters not where you get the capital to launch the product.
- If the product you have is dubious, is not being well made, is costing more to make than the price at which you can sell, and if you have poor workers, you're in trouble even if you do have a good debt-to-equity ratio.

This glaringly simple—and correct—idea comes from Modigliani, who got the Nobel Prize for Economics in 1985.

And it must make you wonder what other ratios are equally unimportant? For example

- Ratio of supervisors to fitters
- Persons per airplane, per shoe, or per ton of cement produced
- Overtime as percentage of basic wages
- Amount spent on training as a percentage of annual turnover
- Research and development spending as a percentage of turnover

You may take three months longer to build and equip a factory, but if you build it cheaper and have a plant that will operate more efficiently than the opposition, with fewer breakdowns, then the speed of completion is not a good measure.

It is clear that whenever we analyze the success of a firm, one conclusion emerges consistently: Success depends on the quality of each and every one of the people, from top to bottom.

Pointless Limits

Do not be frightened by large numbers; by this I mean when your company moves into bigger or higher fields. For example, look at pressures and temperatures used on steam turbines:

- 1000 pounds per square inch pressure
- 1000 degrees Fahrenheit

Such figures used to frighten engineers. They seemed to have a life of their own, whereas the method of measurement is quite arbitrary. Using the metric system, these figures do not look so terrifying:

- 70 atmospheres
- 537 degrees Celsius

It's funny—even those on the metric system are more afraid to exceed 500 degrees Celsius than they are to go to 100 atmospheres pressure!

Within the bounds of safe practice, you should look instead at what is the most economically advantageous figure to use. If you can manage it, take advantage of the research and development done at someone else's expense. When truly tried and proven, then move to use the technology.

Contracts

The arguments in favor of reimbursable contracts are compelling:

"If the job runs behind schedule, we can put another 1000 workers on it to catch up."

"We can start tomorrow rather than awaiting your specifications, which cannot be ready for six months."

But reimbursable contracts are a mixed blessing. The term reimbursable is a euphemism. What it really means is

- Take as long as you wish. If you are a year late, who cares?
- Employ as many people as you like.
- Install whatever equipment you want.
- Do "bogus" productivity deals with workers, pay them beyond all reason, and send me the bill!

Never give your checkbook to anyone else. Get a price for the job (with inflation tied to published indexes for a long-term job).

How do you draw up a contract with another company or individual? Write what you want on one sheet of paper; for example,

- Set a program of construction that I am sure to meet, say, 24 months.
- Ensure that I get paid within 12 days of the end of each month, without fail.
- Get my investment repaid as fast as possible.
- Do not have any take-or-pay clauses.
- Ensure that my firm is not liable in case of breakdown of plant.

Give these requirements to your drafters to write clauses guaranteeing that you get all this.

Do not do it the other way; do not get the drafters to give you a contract document which you read, rewrite, reread, and re-rewrite again until you are satisfied. You may forget or overlook the single most important aspect. Reading heaps of contract documents is soporific; it befuddles the brain. All that unintelligible legal jargon can be overpowering. Adding more and more clauses does not ensure you are getting a better contract.

Productivity

Maybe you could call it a productivity bonus. Did you ever try placing a bet with your counterpart in a contract negotiation? Take a contractor doing a job for you with a schedule of 1st January next. Try placing a bet—not too much, maybe a bottle of bourbon—that the project won't be ready on time. I had to pay up on such a bet recently, but it was with great relief. It meant that a critical job stayed on schedule. Of course, it wasn't the booze that did it. It was pride. By the way, don't claim these kinds of incentives on your expense account!

Stop payment if a supplier is failing to perform. There is nothing that will get results quicker. Also, put a penalty on supplying information by key dates and watch how well that works. The penalty does not need to be large. Back at the supplier's works everyone is threatened that there is "a penalty on this job." The stakes get exaggerated and in the excitement, everyone tries a little harder to give you what you want.

Turnkey or Multicontract Projects

There have been great successes and dismal failures with both turnkey and multicontract projects. It does not matter which you do. Success depends on the management, not on the type of contract. If you have excellent management resources, multicontract projects can prove cheaper. Without such resources, you will have to confine yourself to using one contractor.

Specify Carefully

Be very careful to specify exactly what you want, because that is what you will get. Rather, you certainly will not get more. If you are getting a wall built in the garden, you must say what type and color of blocks should be used—at the inquiry stage. Similarly, if you inquire for a large-scale project like an apartment complex, you must specify everything precisely, from the kind of wall covering that will be used down to the type of adhesive needed to keep the wall covering in place.

Unions

All the nonsense of management versus employees—as if it were a football match—is a myth. Certainly in a free enterprise system it works somewhat as follows. All do not get an equal chance to progress because higher education is available to a smaller percentage of the population than it should be. But you are stuck with those who get the necessary education and it is, for better or worse, from these that you must get your company secretary, your chief designer, your computer programmer, your associate editor, translator, professor, quantity surveyor, electrician, cost accountant, teacher, drafter, or Chief Justice.

Those who, by ill luck or laziness or lack of aptitude for those tasks, are left behind in this race are then branded as "we," whereas those who get through the screen are "they."

You cannot pick someone who has not studied law and make that person Chief Justice—or at least you should not. Nor should you put someone in charge of the financial department of a large company who has not studied and passed all the exams in accountancy.

Unions grew out of the need to protect the exploited masses from the wealthy owners. In a fully developed free enterprise system, the union is now as powerful as practically any organization with which it deals.

A personnel department actually is a friend of the union officials. Every claim brought to a central personnel department is given full attention.

It is a mistake in the first place to have a meeting about such claims as

- Restructuring of sales department
- Shorter working hours
- Higher shift premiums

Once the first meeting is held, the claim is ceded—maybe two years off, but it is ceded to some extent in the future.

All this centralized dealing with what are viewed as "global" or "corporate" problems is destructive. Local management is invited to meetings, put on committees, and thus seen to concur with this process.

But if you have a large personnel department with a dozen persons solely deployed on union claims, what will these people otherwise do? How about having one-quarter the number and just saying no; no meeting, no minutes, no global expansive claim in any way discussed.

When the prosperity of a country is rapidly increasing, better conditions are ceded on such global extras. But in times of recession or normal conditions of moderate growth, the normal countrywide increases are sufficient compensation for the employees, including the boss.

Properly, all claims other than those to keep pace with inflation should be self-financing.

Strikes

There are times of the year when people tend to go on strike; there are times of the year when they are most unlikely to go on strike. There is also a time when people tend to settle a strike.

Look at it like this:

- Who wants to go on strike when saving up for that summer vacation cruise in mid-July?

- Who wants to go on strike just before Christmas, with lots of presents to be bought?

But after Christmas or after the summer vacation season is the silly season. Strikes often begin then. And they often peter out before Christmas for the same reason that they do not begin then.

A project manager I once knew marked up his schedule in green and red showing the "no-strike" and "strike-prone" periods. He never agreed to increases in real income during the "no-strike" periods—he did so only in the danger periods. His plant stayed on schedule without any strikes occurring.

If a manager is going to take a strike, it should be on an issue that he is sure can be won, and can be defended in front of a TV camera.

If an elected official ever gets personally involved in a strike, look out for squalls. He has to settle it quickly—no matter what the consequence for the economy or the firm concerned. Often such officials have no first-hand experience of industrial relations. They think they can wade in and "fix it." What the official is failing to see is that if the problem was that easy to fix, his or her intervention would never have been needed.

Such officials have to keep an eye to the next election. Even at the risk of putting a company out of business in one part of the country, the kudos for fixing a strike will pull some votes in the home constituency.

Economics of Strikes

A general equation can be calculated for the optimum length of strike. Each trade union should do this for its members, instead of mucking along losing money for its unfortunate supporters while pretending to do them a service.

A union calls a strike on average every few years. This depends on the country concerned and the industry.

Now, typically, there are 240 working days in the year. Thus the following is true: The number of working days on strike ÷ the number of years between strikes × 240 must not exceed the extra increase achieved by the strike in the final settlement, or the claimants lose money by making the claim.

This argument assumes, of course, that the strike is not a matter of pride or envy or stupidity or agitation by a group intent on putting the company out of business, or by some political group trying to bring the so-called capitalist system to its knees.

Looking at this result, how many strikes are ever economic? Where are the wonderful successes of the union called strikes? Unions should be made to produce calculations showing the "efficiency" of their efforts, just as managers are expected to produce calculations of the efficiency of their operations. The efficiency of many strikes is zero, and some actually lose money.

Many workers do calculations such as the one above when they return to work following a strike. Management often knows clearly what the result will be, but they're not going to speak out.

There is a critical stage in any strike when it becomes dangerous. This is when it passes the number of days shown above. When it does so, the workers have to press for even higher settlements that are even more impossible to attain. Such strikes go on so long that all lose and they leave a great sense of injustice which the work force will not shake off for years.

One counter to all these arguments is that if pure economics were the only criterion, then the great improvements in the lot of workers would never have been won. True, the arguments given here apply to the ordinary humdrum case and not to those that fall into the category of historic strikes that improve the general lot of workers.

It can be concluded that for a typical case, if the strike extends beyond seven or eight days, the work force will never recoup the loss.

Industrial Relations

Industrial relations is a polite name for management-union arguments and rows.

Let's begin at the beginning. Poor industrial relations will not be everywhere in a sizable firm. It will be excellent in some parts and diabolical in others. Why? Poor or good industrial relations stem from the type of manager in a section or plant.

Watch what happens if you open a new branch office or factory. All depends on the first manager appointed. If that first boss is fair, firm, and efficient, his or her stamp will be there many years later. Even mediocre successors will not be able to destroy the good morale and good performance there.

If, on the other hand, an unfair, unsure, and inefficient manager is first in a new facility, then pity any manager who follows there. It will take at least two years of patient work to get such a place to even mediocre performance.

I once asked a supervisor why everything was well done in the plant where he worked. "Well," he said, "I can put it this way. You can't have some things right and the rest very wrong; for example

- Efficiency
- Cleanliness
- No breakdowns of plant
- Cost of product produced
- No industrial relations problems initiated

All go together—or you have them all wrong." Think about that—all or none surely means that where all these come together is the job that matters, and for a plant, that is on the shoulders of the plant manager.

Thus we conclude that poor industrial relations stem from poor management. This may not be a popular view, as management would like to blame others—shop stewards, union officials, left-wing radicals—anyone but themselves. By and large, management gets the shop stewards and union problems that it deserves.

Look at the problem from the other end. When you joined any firm, were you intent on causing arguments or strikes? Not at all. You know also that none of your friends or contemporaries had such intentions. So if 99 percent of the employees never intend to have confrontation, why do strikes happen? These same employees find themselves driven to it by weak, incompetent management.

Industrial Relations Officers

How do you choose a good industrial relations officer? Obviously the candidate must have been working directly with various categories of workers and have a record of getting on well with them. But something more is needed.

Perhaps a few examples of "outstanding" behavior will help. If you see

- A young supervisor who can laugh with his staff but still turn in the best efficiency on his shift
- A boss who can good-humoredly shout over at an idling group, "Hey, you lazy b.....ds! Get up and at least pretend you are working when my boss is around," and get away without sullen looks
- A person who shows no temper; who is calm and reasonable of voice, even under pressure; who is not overtalkative; and who is not bent on winning every argument or debate
- A person who has the courage to tell all the palatable and unpalatable facts in a hostile situation

there you have an excellent candidate for the industrial relations job. The skilled industrial relations officer knows that you

- Never plan on the assumption that you must win a particular issue by forcing your point of view in toto.
- Never think that the solution lies in either the professed arguments of the union or the management. Very often it is not a compromise of these two but a third solution that is needed.

It is somewhat like crossing a muddy stream on stepping stones in a thick fog. The stones are not in a straight line and there are many which lead nowhere in particular and from which you will have to backtrack. But you always travel one stone at a time.

Only a fool will profess to see the exact spot on the opposite bank at which a landing can be made. At that stage it is really guesswork, and the officials dealing with serious problems are not in the guessing game.

Any person with a bad temper should be kept away from industrial relations. Bad temper is lack of composure and of reason. It is like drunkenness. It is not civilized and is always resented by the audience, so keep your bad-tempered officials locked away.

Negotiating

Never antagonize the moderates in a group or the argument will be interminable.

Never undermine the authority of union headquarters for a short-term settlement that looks clever. On your head be the consequences if, in a dispute, you deal directly with a dissident group which is unofficial. Try to isolate such groups and give the union every chance to solve the problem. Otherwise you are encouraging the formation of a maverick union by proving that the official union is not acting quickly on behalf of the members.

A union team often contains one unreasonable person who keeps butting in with some refrain like "What about our height money?" You can, likewise, include an "unreasonable" negotiator as one of your team. In this way you appear as a reasonable person with whom a deal can be made. The unreasonable one keeps harping on facts that prove your case or on unreasonable acts by the other side such as unofficial stoppages, sit-ins, breaking agreements, wrong statements in claims, even down to grammatical errors.

Do not stay negotiating continuously until 1 o'clock in the morning. Even if it is clear that negotiation will continue for hours. Go home. Leave your team at it. Go to bed and sleep for a few hours. Then return. You will find bloodshot eyes and tense voices still debating. At this point, nonsensical decisions can be made; but you are now fresh and can stem the tide of irrational decisions that can come from debate under pressure and fatigue. Even the most sensible people can be worn down by fatigue.

In all difficult negotiations with unions, or indeed with contractors, always have two representatives so that one can think while the other waffles when the going gets rough.

Managers

Spare a thought for managers. The bad manager is responsible for most problems in industrial relations. If a new facility is put into operation, it will have a crew of enthusiastic workers, but over the years the following pattern may emerge:

- Staff become disenchanted and unhappy.
- They begin to claim more money under various pretexts.
- Eventually a strike develops.

Has such a pattern anything to do with the quality of management? Of course it does.

In the plant with good relations

- People smile when they meet you.
- They are helpful.
- They brag of the good work done in all parts of the plant.

- The plant is the most efficient in the complex.
- The boss sits down with the workers once a week or so and talks with them face to face about how the place is going.

Managers who are good at industrial relations have one thing in common: They can laugh at themselves, and they can get away with having a laugh at the expense of the unions.

Inept managers are always scared out of their wits by a strike so they wade in to "settle" the problem. In their lack of confidence, they believe the boss judges them by the absence of strikes. Thus they tend to give in to totally unreasonable claims.

When this happens, the employees themselves may be as astonished as anyone. It becomes easy for them to tend to see the company as a cow to be milked—and twice a day. Down the slippery slope we go. More and more claims, in and out from picket to sit-in and lockout—a brief breathing space between arguments—a little work in the intervals between stoppages.

If the company has other plants, the disease begins to spread. It spreads also to nearby factories owned by other companies.

There is no cure for this gruesome situation other than to remove the manager. Put in the best manager you have but allow two years to pull things round to even moderate performance.

Is there a protection against such disaster? Yes! Pick top managers to begin with, who have cut their teeth in industrial relations, who have had plenty of practical experience, and who have a good track record. It is too risky to select a top factory manager who has only read about such problems in books. Perfectly reasonable, intelligent, well-dressed, beautiful people can be total disasters in handling the give and take of industrial relations.

Watch that you put a first-class manager in the new big plant. Staff in the largest, most efficient plant tend to get the "swelled-head" syndrome. This passes when the next, even larger, plant is built. But much trouble can emerge if the management vacillates and cannot handle such growing pains.

Any manager who thinks labor peace can be bought is wrong.

When overtime costs are very high, all sorts of irregularities are hidden. If overtime runs at 100 percent, then nobody will notice a small swindle. But if overtime is at 2 percent, then any incorrect allocation—for example, if someone who is taking a day off is also shown at work and is incorrectly paid—will be obvious, because it will distort the week's overtime figures.

I have asked union officials who are excellent at their job to compare industrial relations in various companies. Without exception they compared the managers—not the premises or the products being produced or the working conditions or the remoteness of the factory, and (significantly) not the workers. "Matters in that factory are suicidal. The blinking manager is as thick as the wall. Nobody can get through to him. The workers are sullen and becoming unreasonable. Production is falling off. How I wish a new manager could be appointed." This is a fair summary of the remarks of union officials.

Union officials refer to productivity and watch it just as anxiously as the managers. They know that when the productivity and efficiency are high, this invariably goes with a clever, knowledgeable, and fair manager.

Arbitrators

Spare a thought for arbitrators. When a case reaches arbitration, it is a difficult one and the protagonists have failed to settle it across the table. A chasm has to be crossed and nobody can see where to put the bridge.

When a solution emerges from arbitration, it must have certain characteristics:

- It must seem fair to both sides.
- It must have wide acceptability within each small group comprising the total involved—because group loyalty is stronger than union loyalty.

Arbitrators work to reach a compromise. As their finds must be acceptable, they will tend toward a solution favoring the union. That's where most votes lie. This is to be expected and must be accepted by management as fair. Acceptability is more important than idealistic "absolute" justice, which, in any case, cannot be defined.

Should arbitrators be descended from a long line of extremely successful horse traders? They might come from the trade of "tangler." That is the person who acts as the go-between between buyer and seller at a horse fair in the west of Ireland.

In forming a court or tribunal to hear cases in dispute, bear in mind the following. There should be no lawyers involved. Industrial relations is not a legal game. It is a game of compromise, comparison, and leapfrogging. It requires those skilled in human nature. The court should preferably have as members actual participants so that its findings will be accepted by both parties. If the court comprises, say, three outsiders to a dispute, no party feels bound to its thinking. Having a representative of the participants involved also means that aggravation is stopped while the case goes through hearings; thus you have a sort of "cooling off" period.

The arbitrator's task is very difficult. A member of neither camp, the arbitrator cannot know the total view of either side and must have an unerring feel for the kernel of a problem. A good arbitrator fears no one and should be able to dress down a senior manager or trade union official when this is called for—and it will be. An arbitrator's intent is never more convincing than when he chastises

- The manager—for not speaking clearly, for not answering the query, or for unfair treatment of an employee

- The union official—for coming back with a hoary old claim under a different cloak, for not accepting a reasonable offer, or for not controlling union members while the matter is being judged

If any person can sustain a position of respect from unions and management over a period of five years of active arbitration in a large area, then that is an unusual person. Remember, one blunder, however small, and the arbitrator is sacrificed to either side. It is better to have no arbitrator than one who blunders.

The arbitrator is the last port in a storm—there is nowhere else to go. Thus the arbitrator prevents more strikes and stops more mismanagement than either the union or the top executives.

Cardinal Rules of Chapter 4

DO	DON'T
Strive to keep schedule, budget, and performance all on track	Have patience with poor performers
Plan for possible disasters	Make estimates "from the ground up"
Pick good managers	Aim to have a prestigious project at the expense of other considrations
Allow in your planning for strikes and acts of divine intervention	Use reimbursable contracts
Keep costing simple	
Screen staff to be employed	
Copy the world's best performers	
Specify very carefully	

5

Your Part in the Pyramid

Fair, Firm, and Fast

The three F's is a good way to operate. That's how you would like your boss to work—so why don't you? It's better than the three V's: vain, vague, and vacillating.

No Excuses

Do not let yourself think that other companies

- Are better run
- Can hire and fire at will
- Can introduce change at the drop of a hat
- Have less interference from the government

These are excuses for not doing your job.
  What are the hallmarks of a good manager?

- Courageous
- Confident
- Calm under stress
- Willing to let subordinates have their head
- Communicative at all levels

- Results-oriented; gets excellent results on all aspects of the job

Are You a Coward?

Are you a cowardly manager or supervisor? Do you

- Turn a blind eye to malingering or drunkenness at work
- Let staff come late to work or go home early
- Agree to do away with the time clock
- Give way under pressure to all sorts of minor claims. For example, if one person is doing overtime, do you allow six others to come in so there is no appearance of favoritism? Or if all of one group is then on overtime, do you allow all of several other groups to come in, along with the canteen staff to make them meals?
- Tolerate those who feign sickness so that their colleagues can get overtime (Doing this on a particular day on a shift rota can gain double time for *two* workers, and is thus known as the "double-doubler")

Consider the difficulty of undoing such a mess. You will need a unique manager to do it with a firm, fair hand. Overtime should be reduced from 80 percent to 50 percent in six months, to 25 percent in a year, and down to a normal figure thereafter. Management, by their silly actions, caused the problem, so they must warn employees in advance of what they are going to do.

Don't laugh. Are you sure these games, or similar ones, don't go on in your firm? Check and see the preponderance of "sick" employees on the quick changeover of shifts.

A Host of Other Malpractices

Do you know if any of the following practices occur in your firm?

- Employees who clock in for friends.
- Some clock out for friends who go home early when overtime is being worked (supervision is weaker then). Supervisors are used to these practices because they inherited them 20 years ago.
- Overtime is allocated to those who pay for beer at a local pub for the boss of a section.
- Overtime is paid to equal last year's total, whether worked or not.

- All overtime is shared between an elite few—and no replacements are brought in—all this while there is unemployment in the country.
- People on night duty take turns to sneak away for a nap.
- Equipment is stolen from the stores.
- Staff gets bogus doctor's certificates to allow them to stay away from work.
- Machinery is operated inefficiently, with parts broken or malfunctioning.
- People are unfriendly toward each other.
- The work force has no knowledge of the status of the firm, its plans, and its prospects.

If you have some or all of these malpractices in your firm, have you the guts to do something about it? Or, instead of recognizing such warts, do you go off attending seminars and courses on "management," esoteric topics that do not stoop to look at the worms under the stones.

Maybe you should stay at work and go out there and cure all the diseases. The courses can wait until you have warded off all the threats of bankruptcy.

There is an old saying: "Look after the cents, and the dollars will look after themselves." Well, apply that adage. I admit it is not easy or comfortable. It leads to confrontation, maybe a strike, or bad publicity. Will your boss support your actions? You must persuade her to do so and not to weaken if a major row develops, with TV coverage and pointed questions thrown at her.

Okay, it was the weak management of 10–50 years that allowed the bad practices to creep in. But it is your number-one task to eliminate them.

Please do not praise this book to a friend and then avoid or delay doing something about malpractices in your firm. None mentioned here may be rife, but don't pretend that none exist.

The People You Work With

Why do we fear telling colleagues about their mistakes? You don't have to be smart about it or write to them formally. Just tip them off. Maybe then they will do the same for you and save you the time spent eliminating the last vestiges of trifling error from your efforts. This way, you and your colleagues will be more effective as a group. It's not the absence of small errors, but the mass of effective, practical, and economic improvements you can achieve that counts. If you were infallible, you certainly would not be, at your age, in the post you now hold.

Do not forget that you get very little done except through other people. Thus the way you relate to all your colleagues and subordinates and bosses is the single most important attribute you can have. The "I am not paid to be nice to people" attitude is the antithesis of the correct one.

Attitude Shaping

Think of the capable people you know. They all have one fine quality—composure. They are confident that they know what they are doing—and they do know.

The advice given by Australian John Landy to a young Irish miler (Ron Delaney) is sound advice for us all: "Relax! Don't fight against it, breathe regularly, don't use energy slowing yourself down." Delaney had quality but he was trying so hard he was tired before a race was half over. He subsequently won the 1500 meter Olympic race with his friend Landy on his heels. Landy had injured his foot the previous day, never said a word about it, and was first to congratulate Delaney.

This incident has a moral regarding your attitudes to colleagues at work. Be friendly. Help them if you can. Life is not such a rat race that you cannot take pleasure watching a cohort win. If you've helped, you will be the more pleased to extend congratulations.

Relaxed, you are in control of a situation. You have the main objectives in mind. Bumping, boring, passing, or boxing in will not panic you.

Don't spend too much of your time with subordinates who work near you. This gives remoter staff the impression that you have an inner court for favorites. Indeed, such "inner courts" are often comprised of "thinkers," who are not involved in the part of a business that makes or breaks it.

Don't trust anyone who calls you "Madam" or "Sir"; it is not warranted. Remember the beggars whose "Sirs" are followed by flowery curses when alms are not forthcoming. Some people are polite not because you deserve it but because it suits their purpose.

Never forget that youth tends to see older persons as

- Hidebound and hiding behind red tape
- Lacking in initiative
- Having shipped oars awaiting retirement
- "Schoolteachers" spotting and gloating over misspellings, but not involved themselves in essay-writing

Never a Kind Word

Don't be critical of other departments. You've known the person whose conversation is laden with comments like

"That 'bimbo' in Personnel"

"I've told those nitwits a dozen times..."

Everyone is out of step except Johnny.

You must learn to get along with those around you. Sure, they are an odd lot, but that's what you have to play with. Did it ever occur to you to wonder how they view you?

Naturally, the flaws in the performance of your colleagues become clearer and clearer the longer you work with them:

- One is an empire builder.

- Another is a gossiper, criticizing all around.

- A third is perpetually laying the blame on other parts of the organization.

- One thinks all her goats are sheep.

- There is a touch of the braggart in the fifth.

- The lecturer on every topic is a bore.

- The smart aleck uses her knowledge to trip up colleagues.

- The lazy one does not pull his weight.

You can obsess about all this, but you can't really tell any of them what you think. Can you? Or even give them a broad hint, because they will resent that.

What if they focused exclusively on your faults and how irritating you are? Think of all the things they would probably like to say to you.

So dwell a while on the positive, cooperative, friendly, effective, dynamic, innovative, courageous, efficient things they all do, and get on with doing your own job a bit better.

We All Make Mistakes

Climb down. If you are wrong, say so, like this:

"Sorry, I got that wrong. Tom Ryan checked my calculations and found them in error. Here are the correct figures."

Is that so hard?

If you ever make a glaring mistake by publicly advocating something that is nonsensical to a section of your staff, what will happen? If it is something all of them know is wrong, something that you just never learned, then they will growl and complain ever afterwards that you don't know what you are talking about. The only way you can gain their respect is to go back and admit you were wrong, and that it has been pointed out to you. If you can swallow your pride and do this, maybe your staff will relent and say "Well, he's educable at least; maybe he deserves another chance."

This approach has several advantages:

- Knowing someone will quickly spot any error and that you must beat them to the punch keeps you on your toes.

- Your staff can learn by your example. They won't have to pull their hair out to ensure 100 percent accuracy in everything they send to you. They now know that they can follow up with a phone call to amend a figure without any loss of face.

Make it clear to your staff that they should not stay silent if they think you are advocating an incorrect line of action—even if you previously issued it as an order or policy.

If something ambiguous or erroneous comes your way from colleagues, don't be smart and think you'll have a couple of months worth of jokes and sarcasm at their expense. "Let's see now, Jerry, you're requesting $25,000 to replace all the Personnel Department's old typewriters with PC's. And Sally, you've budgeted $5000 for a three-year supply of ribbons for those same typewriters. Who's coordinating the budget down there, Elmer Fudd?"

Come off it. Be a help. Find out which is right and just do it.

Always give people a way out, an escape, like a "spot the deliberate error" contest. If you don't leave an exit, you may corner a rat who will fight as if her life were on the line. As any matador (who's still alive) will tell you, "Always leave the bull a place to go."

Ego Trips Come in a Variety of Colors

You've met the egoist who regularly criticizes everyone: "I never thought much of

- General de Gaulle
- Ronald Reagan

- John F. Kennedy
- Winston Churchill
- You (when you are not listening)

This is an attempt to elevate oneself, to gain status by disparaging the persons and/or lifestyles of the rich and famous. Recognizing and accepting how clever they are, or were, would widen the gap and aggravate the jealousy.

The "squirrel" that hoards information thinks no one else can do the job. He is not effective, because he acts alone and has little help from colleagues. In the extreme, this behavior is called the "black-hole syndrome"—vast quantities of information are absorbed into the void without any feedback coming out under any circumstances. Colleagues get tired making allowances for such behavior and eventually will leave the squirrel to hibernate.

You must be able to prove that you are training your immediate subordinates properly. When you have done so, you can be fired without any bad effect on the performance of the firm. If you fear this, then you must have little confidence that you yourself are being groomed to move up—to displace your boss! Be prepared to take the risk, or you have no courage or genuine ability to go further.

If you have to lean very heavily on someone, but then see her being successful in a job unconnected with your bailiwick, congratulate her anyway. She may appreciate the fact that you can admire her work in one area but will still push her to give the service needed in your area. Your job may be something she just doesn't like doing.

Watch your use of the word "I." Anyone who uses it consistently in speech or writing is trying to highlight their role as singular. Granted, it is exciting to get into a position in which you have some influence, but there's something childish about allowing the ego to run unchecked.

Some people are so egotistical that whenever you try to discuss a problem with them, the conversation inevitably becomes a dissertation on the innovation, creativity, and determination they showed in solving a different problem. Every problem put to them seems to have its analogy in some clever thing they think they did a year ago. Yawn.

You may be proud of something you have done, but you may have cribbed it or got the right answer by incorrect methods. You may be pleased in the same way as a dog that catches a rabbit—pleased she made no mistakes this time. Don't be over-proud of anything you have personally done.

Model Behavior

Leave tasks to those who should do them. If they make a mess, tell them what was wrong. If they mess it up again, do it yourself. Don't say a word. When they find out, they will be hopping mad and will fire alarm rockets in all directions. Sit tight; say nothing. If they get on their bicycles and do it right the third time around, let them have the job back, but not otherwise.

If they insist, via your boss, that you should not interfere, write a "mea culpa" note, but when the need arises, repeat the treatment. Mea culpa notes cost little to write and allow you to get the job done. Your boss should be well pleased, having noted that you apologized and at the same time got results. One or two such efforts and your colleagues will get that much more efficient, as they will fear losing their jobs.

A boss who is inefficient or wrong loses the respect of staff—forever. It's like a dial on a control panel that does not read correctly for some years. Even if a maintenance person says it's now okay, people will continue to work around it because they've all grown accustomed to doing without it.

So, the way to stay influential is to be right. There was a game we played as kids called "king of the hill." Any kid that got on top of a heap of sand or a high hillock would, in this game, dare anyone to "knock me down."

Some managers behave like this. When they get on top of a small empire, they begin to send off salvoes like

"I want this done by 2 o'clock."

"I ordered that to be done yesterday; why isn't it done?"

Some advocate being forceful and aggressive to maintain control. No. You get the respect you deserve.

"Don't catch the hand of a drowning man," is an old saying. Instead, throw a lifebelt on the end of a rope. Someone who is drowning will drag you down as well, but if you throw a lifebelt, you can't be accused of not helping. In fact, now the person has a chance of reaching the shore. Otherwise, two would have drowned instead of one.

The Importance of Alibis

For the kind of manager who likes to keep everything vague and fluid (and then reneges when the pressure is on), keep a written record of all agreements made, and let him or her know you are doing so. For example, as you're making your plans by phone, be writing! "Agreed. You will send me so-and-so by next week." Then pop it in the tray for typing as the pleasantries of signing off are in progress. Don't bother doing this with managers who always keep their word on agreements. For them, just jot down somewhere in the file what was agreed (in case you are away and someone wants to know the score).

If anyone quotes an authority higher than you as the reason for nonaction, be suspicious. That higher authority may not know what you know. So find out! Having learned that this dodge won't work, the procrastinator won't try it on you again (but may try it on others).

Never trust the words "It is Company policy." On what basis did the "Company" decide? Did the "Company" ever see the problem at all? People rely on the capital C in company or the capital B in board to discourage further probing. But consider this: No board would con- sciously decide in favor of inefficiency, waste of resources, duplication of effort, or stupidity. Worst of all is "The management committee decided." If the managers meet weekly, the number of different rumors that emerge as to what was "decided" will match pretty exactly the number of managers who advocate a certain line. Take instructions through proper channels only, not from rumors as to what is reputed to have occurred, and do not act on rumors of committee decisions.

Areas of Responsibility

Do not

- Waste your time on demarcation disputes with other managers
- Patrol your section, flushing out and attacking interlopers

It's unavoidable that sometimes you end up working on someone else's turf. Some managers, as a matter of course, will make life hell by objecting to every single thing that even vaguely impinges on their province. To get on with your work and silence these objections, give any such objector a signed note certifying that the item which is the source of the complaint is entirely your idea and responsibility, and then bash ahead.

Don't unduly encroach on other managers' staff or province. If you consider someone for promotion, check with that person's boss first and you may find that she is up for promotion in any case, prefers where she is, and was only interested in your territory as a poor second. So pick someone else.

Change for the Sake of Change

Try to avoid the "golf club captain" approach to management. The golf club captain's office is for one year. What can one contribute in just a year? To leave a mark, a captain's options are pretty much limited to

- Extending the locker room
- Moving the 6th green
- Planting some trees
- Adding a bunker on the 18th fairway
- Extending the parking lot

    This syndrome leads a manager to

- Open new—uneconomic—outlets
- Build a new office block (according to Parkinson)
- Launch a glossy magazine to go to all customers
- Paint all vans a new color

    It's all a matter of change for change's sake. Beware. It may come to be known as "Kelly's" folly.

Piercing the Veil

If you are a bank branch manager, or a shop manager or plant manager, you must not retreat into your office "fortress," never to be seen by the rest of the staff. If you do, you will give the impression of being afraid of what may be brought to your attention. You will seem "besieged." Do you think that because you're invisible, problems will be invisible too? They may be, but only to you. So be seen; get out.

Never prevent anyone doing something because it may fail and reflect badly on you. The person trying the development has probably studied it in depth and is prepared to have a go at the expense of his or her own reputation.

Take a leaf from New York Mayor Koch's book. When "No" is the proper answer, say "No." For example,

- When there is no money to do it
- When it is not a sound economic investment
- When it is throwing money away just to be popular or kind

Get to know two or three clear-minded people off whom you can bounce ideas. They need not be from your own department or division, nor need they even be in your company. Only about 1 percent of managers have access to such an invaluable "objectivity" tool for testing the truth. When such a partnership operates both ways, each seeking advice on occasion from the other, it is one of the most valuable assets possible for effective action.

Don't confuse issues with technical gobbledygook...

"Of course, the osmotic superfluity of the reverse component precludes the use of..."

This is oneupmanship. It's a waste of time. Anyone who professes to agree with you is probably an ass. Sooner or later, someone is going to get the real picture, and the more you prevaricate, the more suspicion you generate, and the more people drool to take you down a peg because you are so uppity with your jargon. If you can't make a presentation clear to your colleagues, you must not know your subject, or maybe you are hiding something to con them into a particular line of action. Whenever someone else reverts to jargon in talking to you, look out. You've touched a nerve.

Euphemisms

Beware the euphemism. Some terms and concepts take on meaning beyond what was originally intended for them:

Absenteeism—as if it is an unavoidable disease, like an aneurysm. It implies that nobody is ever AWOL.

Overhead—this consists of all the costs not directly related to work at hand. Everybody watches carefully how long or how much it takes to produce a tire or a wheelbarrow; but the unseen "overhead" consists of the people watching and measuring. Who measures them?

Productivity index—a measurement made while you avoid taking the obvious step of reducing the crew size.

Company Structure

Don't allow your personnel department to "rationalize pay scales." What this will do is upgrade lots of people. Also, it usually ends up equating the pay of many diverse categories by reducing the number of categories. With modern computers, you are better off having many pay scales. Few can then equate with other more powerful groups.

Any move to rationalize pay scales or restructure category levels will be eagerly accepted by your personnel people. It justifies their existence. They have read books about it. It will be purely a question of negotiation between personnel and the union officials—ordinary managers do not care or know about such important matters.

Examine the organizational structure to see if any level is contributing little or nothing. In a changing world, a certain amount of obsolescence is unavoidable; but deadwood can also result because of the "incumbency syndrome," or stagnation. Some jobs lose their importance. In either case, don't try to protect the image of the post. Expose it to rough weather. Make it work. If incumbents have grown complacent, shape them up or ship them out. If you have the power, and if the post is obsolete, do away with it. The respect and credibility gained is worth the pain of change. Believe it. Everybody knows when a manager or a post is useless.

Take a look at what your managers actually do. If their sole contribution is checking the work of others and passing largely negative comment or delaying the work, then theirs is a "non-job." If you have authority levels somewhat as follows:

Level A approves $500,000

Level B approves $50,000

Level C approves $5000

Level D approves $500

Look at the instant economies realized by eliminating entirely Level C (you probably have four of them for every A). All you have to do is restructure the authority levels and redistribute the responsibilities and C is out of a job.

Have at least six to ten people reporting to each and every manager. Then each manager will be busy enough to keep her nose out of any individual area. If you have an operating manager with only one or two reporting to her, she won't be busy enough and will interfere, half run, or undo their jobs.

Never have an in-line—in-the-way—assistant. You will drive the person round the bend trying to keep tabs on what goes on below him. Such an in-line assistant will be a "gofer" most of the year and then go crazy with activity during your vacations. Did you ever hear a group of such "assistants" describing their jobs? They live their years out waiting to get into a position in which they can at last do something.

Give all assistants a specific written area of responsibility, and keep clear of it. A good division of labor is to leave operations and short-term work to assistants and keep long-term work for yourself.

Nobody should have two bosses. It is human nature to back one horse only. Likewise, an employee will serve one boss to the virtual exclusion of the other, or he will serve neither. When one boss looks for services, the man will claim he is busy for the second—in effect, he is opting out of an impossible situation.

Tasks requested by, or required to be done for, outsiders should be estimated in work-days and with target dates (with the agreement of both sections). This will eliminate the cuckoo who never hatches eggs.

Line, Functional, and Staff

There is no great mystery about these terms. They fade in and out of fashion. But let us examine what they mean.

If your firm consists of just one factory or office, then nearly everything seems to be directly in-line management. Even within this one facility you have something like this:

- All wages controlled and paid from one center
- Costing from one office
- Centralized purchasing
- Sales run from one office
- Personnel matters with another office

Line control is normally very clear, for example

Rank and file to foreman, or floor supervisor

to supervisor of production works

to senior-level manager

to general manager

Functional is the work done by a section which

- Sets standards
- Issues operating instructions, including safety instructions
- Monitors to ensure instructions are all applied correctly

A functional section is only needed in a company that has several separate factories or branches. It is not economic or wise to have a separate group at each branch to carry out all functions—so one central functional section is set up. This section does work under the direction of the common boss of the section and all the branches. In this way this functional control is exercised on behalf of that boss.

Typical examples are

- The headquarters accounting section
- The personnel section

Staff officers working in the office of, say, the chief engineer, carrying out tasks at his behest, are more transitory. Their existence or demise depends on what the chief engineer wants done and how often.

The Reorganization Charade

There is an affliction among some managers that manifests itself in the regular output of reorganization proposals. It's an excuse for action, it seems, for managers who either have nothing better to do or who are avoiding doing it.

"As soon as we get organized properly, we can work wonders."

Such proposals are usually very complex and backed up by elaborate job specifications.

The organizational diagram does not matter a whit. This is not popular to say, but consider for a moment:

- If you have a beautiful organizational diagram, with marvelous job specifications, and into the little boxes you insert all the incompetents you work with, what will happen?
- If, on the other hand, you pick all the best and smartest people you know and put them to work in a loosely defined organization, leaving them to decide for themselves where to focus and examine and expand, you can put your organizational charts where the sun don't shine.

"But this department has not had a reorganization for eleven years."

It's a telling argument. The implication is that we must move forward and surely the organization which suited in the past cannot possibly suit in the modern world, with all the advances made in the meanwhile. Be careful.

Studying the "design" of organizations is an amusing exercise. You hear talk of

- Open and closed systems
- Rational organizations
- Centralization and decentralization
- Divisionalization
- Adhocracy
- Bureaucracy

Such concepts hold a certain "intellectual" fascination—divorced from reality. They are so indefinite that theories can abound as to their application or development. Leave such investigations to those who don't have any work to do. It is simpler and more productive to ignore such exercises as diversionary and to concentrate on getting good people.

If an organization is not functioning, the real reason may well be that there is some deadwood there. Cut it out, and have no reorganization. In many countries you cannot fire people who have been in a company more than a year. If this applies, put your nonperformers on some "special duty," until you can perhaps get them to quit. It is often useful to push someone sideways and manufacture a bogus job, but beware losing control of the useless activity that will follow.

Just because you meet another manager from a sister company who has done some major reorganization, such as centralizing or decentralizing, it is no reason to rush off and do the same. In the U.K. some managers do things to get in the Honors List (even to become Lords!), even if the results are a disaster. Doing something without being certain of the benefits is irresponsible. If a person's actions are motivated by self-aggrandizement, the actual benefits reaped will be about half of what they claimed, and a year later than projected. Some managers jeer at their colleagues just for sport: "You mean to say you are still centralized. We have only five people in our corporate headquarters." Don't rush off to prove you can do it as well.

Consultants

It is very difficult for a company to effect a major reorganization without using outside consultants. Many of us have performed in this capacity for other firms, and then have turned around and hired outsiders to do it for our own firm. There is some logic in this: The use of an outsider gives an air of objectivity.

Who would believe that old Fred Smith from our own personnel department could and would interview us all objectively and say what should be done. But if it's Zalon Sarkoviki from Cincinnati, that's an entirely different matter. At 29, Sarkoviki will have a fresh viewpoint. Look at his first-class degree in Parapsychology, and his masters in Brain Draining, and his doctorate in Interpersonal Relations. Don't carp on the fact that he didn't leave college till he was 28. Where did he meet any "real people" along the way?

It's true. By interviewing all managers (preferably accompanied by one from within the firm), the whole exercise seems fair and as objective as a reorganization can be made to appear.

The board of a German manufacturing company that was quite successful called in management consultants. The general manager was surprised. He got the curriculum vitae of the four consultants assigned to the study and found

- None was over 30 years old.

- None had ever had anything to do with manufacturing industry.

- None had held any one position for more than two years; two of them had not held a job for more than 12 consecutive months.

He was incensed and wrote all this to his board. They seemed to think it was an advantage that the consultant not know too much about the business and argued that this made them more objective. This argument is put forward by those whose purpose it suits. The ultimate example of that nonsense would be to breed a group of people on a remote island (we have a few uninhabited islands off Ireland that would be suitable), thus ensuring they have no experience whatever and can be 100 percent objective! Teach them mathematics, psychology, organization theory, science—but don't let them do anything.

Government officials are a good example of the application of this theory. They never put a medical doctor in charge of the Department of Health or an engineer in charge of the Department of Industry. Not at all, the doctor takes over Industry, and the engineer Health—thus both can be very objective. To make sure they stay objective, the ministers are moved around every two years or so. This may give the appearance of dynamic leadership, but it is really to move some of the "objective" ministers away from the mess they are causing. In the meantime, the people changing jobs every year or two are gaining great experience for some eventual brilliant work. Before that can happen, you can be sure another government will take over.

So, the study was done, a reorganization advocated—which split the general manager's job in two, forming joint general managers. If you ever see this in a company, it is a sign that the board cannot make up its mind who should run the firm, or it is a firm that is making money despite the board. When news spread around Europe, the original general manager was offered a job as sole general manager of an even bigger firm in France—an arch-competitor of the German firm—and he went there and stole several large markets for the French.

The probable reason for the exercise was that the board had lost confidence in their general manager—or began to dislike him.

No doubt many readers will have read Lee Iacocca's biography. When Henry Ford II called in management consultants, the resulting reorganization split Iacocca's job in two. Later Iacocca was edged out altogether. This is a lesson in the use of management consultants.

The boss does not call in management consultants and give them a free hand. First, he describes to them the problem areas in the organization—as he sees it. Then, magically, the consultants will focus on those areas and perhaps come up with solutions more in line with the boss's views.

If any objections appear, the top-class management consultant will plead that consulting is an art, not a science—by which is meant that there is no logic to what is being done. Rather, what is being done looks beautiful to the management consultant because that is what she has been encouraged to do.

"I shall be very surprised if your investigations do not address the problem in such-and-such an area" is how the consultant is usually set working. "I'm not prejudging your findings, but you should consider, among other options, doing away with such-and-such and merging that other task." Ever hear that "whoever pays the piper calls the tune?"

The following passage, possibly, but probably not, written by some Roman (erroneously attributed to Petronius) shows that the reorganization plague has been with us for some time:

> We trained hard but it seemed that every time we were beginning to form up into teams we would be reorganized. I was to learn later in life that we tend to meet any new situation by reorganizing and a wonderful method it can be for creating the illusion of progress while producing confusion, inefficiency, demoralization, and despair.

Management consultants for the Roman army! How about that!

Technical consultants are an entirely different question. Here you are looking for a technical expertise that is not in your firm. Maybe it's a geologist, or a seismic expert. That is fine, but there is a caveat. In a case where you seek a "second opinion" on a design being done in your firm for the first time, there is a danger. If you have a design department, ensure that it does its own analysis and conclusions without the advice of the outside technical consultant. In this way you're attacking the problem on two fronts. I've seen cases where the only failure on a project was where the firm's design team left one portion entirely in the hands of the outsider; they were very busy and diligent on all the rest of the project. "All should be well. We have an international expert team of consultants on that problem. Why second guess them?" So, have it done by your own team and see if they come up with anything that the consultant has not spotted.

Do not second guess your key staff. If you have a design department headed by a chief electrical engineer, do not continue to second guess her by hiring consultants to report to you. Persuade your chief to hire any necessary consultants to report to her—and if they are needed you should be able to muster the arguments to get this done.

You may hire a consultant over the head of your staff once in a decade, but you must have very sound and understandable reasons for doing so.

Otherwise, you lose the confidence of the entire design staff. Why should they put themselves out if you are going to let some outsider come in, who you listen to all too readily, and to whom you pay big bucks for the advice. It's not surprising that they would cease to try. And now you'll need to get consultants regularly. It's the worst of both worlds—you have a department that is useless and you pay large sums to outsiders to do the work that the department should do.

It is tempting to have consultants because if things go wrong, it can be blamed on the bad advice given by the consultant—not on you. Consultants should never be used to relieve you of your responsibilities.

Reorganizations can often get bogged down by resistance of local managers and unions. A little "lubrication" may follow— in the form of extra staff or promotions—and the flow of reorganization resumes.

It is not rare for consultants to end their reports with problems that remain to be solved—very careful not to say that they can solve them. Indeed, the bonus of doing a study is often the extra business dragged in after the main task is done.

Know in advance what will emerge when you hire consultants. For example, if you hire consultants to examine the "communication systems" in your firm, what will emerge? It is obvious:

- The consultants must have a track record of installing information systems. Otherwise you would not hire them.
- They will display their wares by bringing your people to talk to two or three satisfied customers who are using a complete system designed by the consultants.
- Your representatives will think that all progressive firms have such a scheme. They will not go to look at two or three other firms that are

performing better than those visited, but that do not use such a scheme.

- A new section will be permanently set up and the system installed in your firm.
- Improvements will occur at a leisurely pace; the new section does not want to work itself out of a job.
- You can never dismantle this new miniempire.

If that is what you want and plan to do, and if in your judgment it will be an efficient move, go ahead.

A firm in Wales did what is described above. Three years later they hired a different consultant to review progress. Obviously, they were beginning to entertain second thoughts. One consultant will rarely run down another; after all, they live off each other's efforts. The second reported, in a suitably convoluted report, that no progress had occurred other than things that would have happened in any case just as quickly.

Trimming the Fat

Watch proposed changes in organization, centralization or decentralization, delegation or standardization, or so-called productivity deals. It is often merely the spread of Parkinson's Law: more people added, none subtracted, even though before the change many were purported to be wasting time.

When and How to Reorganize

It's easy. Do not wait and wait and then have a big "reorganization." Knock off or add what you should as you go. If you set out to do one huge reorganization, managers will defer decisions and delay improvements, pending the outcome. You provide a great excuse for temporary inactivity. During such a phase the indicators of success in the firm will usually drop.

Don't take the word of senior managers that everyone is busy and more staff needed. Give credibility to the person who has reduced staff in certain areas, not to the one who is always pressing for increases. Better still, go and sit down for a day or two in this so-called busy office. The threat to do so often quells the expansionist ideas.

Cut out posts which exist only to

- Coordinate

- Liaise

- Cooperate

If the staff can't coordinate, liaise, or cooperate without an intermediary, it's time something was done. If you need a specialist, have nobody reporting to her and pay her on a scale suited to the specific nature of the job. This will prevent empire building in an effort to up the salary. Don't make the mistake of having a specialist without a full day's pressing problems. Having recorded everything on which she is expert, don't let her sit admiring her handiwork.

Avoid a military-type organizational structure; everyone will fight to get more and more assistants. Armies had to have officers in reserve to provide replacements as warriors were mown down (someone had to issue orders to shove more fighters into the breach). This practice has crept into the business world as well. Officers allow warriors to be mown down whenever battle is joined, claiming that their delegation is so good that they need not check every detail. They argue that it would be foolish to sack the officer if the warrior is not a good swordsman.

Before restructuring a group, consult everyone who will be in the new set-up and have them write what they think would be the correct structure. About 95 percent will pen something close to what you want to do. You can use this to silence the 5 percent of grumblers who support the status quo.

Benefits of a Reorganization

It is not, of course, all black and white. If the whole organization is upended, then some benefits can accrue, provided that full advantage is taken of the opportunity. For example, the headquarters can be moved 200 miles away so that employees can be radically reduced—because many will not want to move. Nobody who had a post in the old organization has any claim on a post in the new one. Each position from top to bottom can be opened, advertised, and filled. In this way, all persons who have passed their prime or who have burned out can be left as extras or supernumeraries.

You can end up with all the best people in the key jobs—and this fact is what will make a firm hum, rather than the shape of the organization (which most people believe is the sole reason).

Making Success Easier

Never leave a dud for longer than two years in any post. A dud for two years is a dud forever. The dud's subordinates will keep up hopes of improvement for a year or so, but disillusionment and disinterest will set in, and this will kill effort and initiative.

Do not depend upon study groups and seminars and conferences to solve management problems.

As an example, take the problem of absenteeism. You can send supervisors on courses showing them statistics and trends and the latest psychological advances, but is this the best course of action?

A parable: There once was a supervisor named Erin in a plant with the worst absenteeism in the company. One day, Erin stopped the general manager and asked if the general manager would do her a favor. The general manager, knowing Erin to be a person of high integrity, said yes, even before knowing what the favor was. Erin then asked respectfully why the company couldn't stop these managerial improvement courses and just fire the greatest malingerer in the plant. "Just watch what happens to the statistics," she said. She was hacked off at having to "make cups of tea" for such people, ask about the kids and the missus... Erin's favor was granted. Two were let go and absenteeism at the plant halved in three months.

Remember that the Erins of the world grow frustrated and disappointed watching all this theoretical nonsense while the 1 percent dodgers get away without punishment. You may break the hearts of the good 99 percent with your lecture sessions.

When a job is going to be worth more because of new responsibilities, but the incumbent is not competent to do it properly, retitle the job and put a new person in.

Never organize or reorganize on a permanent basis to suit the problem employee. In a business setting, the causes of problems are usually widely known, and if you don't face it and put the incompetents where they rightfully belong, you can kill initiative for a long time in a department. A poor golfer who plays badly in front of many aspiring players, however new to the game, can slow up an entire course. If you don't make it so that aspirants of better quality can "play through," they will leave the course.

If your organizational structure was in place before you came along, it's easy to opt out of

- Removing incompetents
- Changing structures where wrong
- Cutting off out-of-date and obsolete areas

Admittedly, it's far easier when starting with a clean sheet. But no excuses, please. Just do what you have to do.

You may be tempted, now and then, to promote staff just to keep a pot from boiling over. This is a short-term solution, encourages repeat boiling, and discourages staff from having a go somewhere else and from widening their horizons. The inclination of most of us is to stay put and hope to get more money doing the one job better and better. We should be encouraged to break out of the cocoon and fly by ourselves. Promising young people, remaining in a protected atmosphere, may never live up to their promise.

It's like training dogs. Raise a fool of a dog that can't catch a rat if it ran over his paws and you'll never turn him into a ratter. But train a pup as a ratter from the start and he will be valuable. It is better to have a few good ratters than a hundred fools.

Producing Standards

Produce standards for anything that has to be done regularly:

- Specifications
- Designs
- Drawings

This reduces the damage the know-it-all boss can do who squirrels away all sorts of information in his drawer or in his head, waiting to pounce on an unfortunate, unknowing, unsuspecting subordinate.

To prevent senior staff from perpetually passing caustic comments on junior staff's work, insist that operations manuals be prepared.

These manuals should also record common pitfalls to watch out for and past errors. Detail one person to produce each such manual. A draft should be submitted to selected managers with experience in the particular field for detailed comment. Then produce the final version.

Once this has been done for all aspects of the work, young recruits can operate with more confidence. If a boss tries the game of "we tried that in 1972 but it didn't work," the junior can quote from more accurate, objective records.

This scheme may provide less fun for those who like starting a job from scratch, hoping to put their imprint on an accepted change, but it is a surer method of operation in the long run.

Get policies set on anything you can and then avoid all the hundreds of specific cases relying on precedent.

The Long and Short of Staffing

If you have a surplus of staff, there will be no need to cosset them. After all, you can get a job done by any of two or three persons. But if you are tight for staff, you must get full utilization by encouraging, helping, appreciating, facilitating, and even liking. So the tighter you are for staff, the better you will utilize them, the better you will treat them, the better you will cooperate with and like them.

You have, no doubt, been handed the we-have-recommended-an-increase-in-staff-to-do-this-work-but-not-having-got-it-how-can-management-expect-work-done argument. Logically extended, to do nothing, all that's necessary is to keep pressing for more and more staff.

There is no optimum or correct number in any team. It's all a matter of judgment. With fewer people than before, you have to make decisions faster, with fewer facts and with greater risk of missing the optimum solution and improvements. With more people, you run the risk of underemploying your staff.

The our-establishment-has-not-been-properly-staffed-in-the-past-five-years-how-can-we-be-expected-to-produce-results complaint simply indicates that the establishment should be cut back.

If one group has not done essential work, pleading lack of staff, write and ask that the work be sent to you. Ask the boss of that unit if he's willing to wager on whether you will do it all as well as your own job in one week. Chances are, you will never get the work to do. The initial reaction will be: "Send the lot to the *!#*x! That will soften her cough." But if you have a reputation as a fantastic worker, the fear will set in that you just might do it and make them look foolish. Besides, the worst that can happen is that you'll see first-hand that they really do need the extra help.

If someone does not want to do something they will rationalize it. If you are looking for volunteers to go to Alaska drilling for oil and one applicant says, "I'd love to go, but first I want to know the following details..." you need hardly listen further. That person is not going. Out comes a list of 20 extenuating factors—from temperatures to kit allowances, annual holidays, married or single status...

This applicant may not know it, but what is actually being sought is a reason not to go. "I'd have gone except for the miserable kit allowance." If someone wants to go, the answer is simply "yes." All the details are normal. What applies to everyone else who goes is okay.

Watch out for such rationalizing at interviews when hiring. Those who feel they must apply but don't want the job rationalize themselves out of the race—a foolish thing to do, because the poor interview will be remembered.

Every person in a routine production job should have a fall-back project that can be used to develop talents and experience and to improve and develop that person's area of activity. This is a bonus to the company as well as to the individual. These projects help employees to prove their worth over and above running their routine jobs well. But watch that the primary job gets priority.

Use every skill available. If you are scared of letting an accountant or actuary or engineer pry into your field, then you don't deserve to last. If you have the qualities required for the job, nobody can oust you. If you use experts fully, your whole field benefits.

Don't leave well-qualified people to grow bored doing a job that has been fully developed to the stage where technicians can run it.

Management Diseases

Waves of management diseases spread across the world. Most of them originate in the United States. Schools and universities watch out for the latest innovations in management. They must not be left behind by other such institutions. Enthusiasm for the new disease is followed within a few months—usually not more than a couple of years—by disillusionment and rejection. However, "inoculation" against one strain does not serve to prevent severe attacks by the next strain to come along.

Some of the strains of "managementitis" are

- Job Evaluation
- Management by Objective
- Attitude Surveys
- Parasitic Units
- Productivity Agreements
- Transaction Review

Let's consider these. You may discover others (usually after they have ravaged your firm).

Job Evaluation

It makes great sense—on paper. "Pay should be tied to the actual job done." "How can anyone do the job unless it is properly described?" Thus are you sold the idea of Job Evaluation.

Be forewarned that

- Introducing Job Evaluation will increase the scale of pay for a significant percentage of the employees affected by the scheme.
- Many people's time will be tied up serving the scheme—far beyond what such a project deserves.

- The boss of the person submitting a job description has a direct interest in seeing the subordinate get a good score, thus tending to push up the pay of that same boss. Thus if you are forced to have job evaluation, do not allow any supervisor to approve the job descriptions of their immediate subordinates. Put the reviewing at least one step higher.

Reading the job descriptions will make you wonder what any supervisor has left to do if the subordinate does what is written. Indeed, it will make you wonder what you can do, because you will frequently find that your job (and maybe even your boss's job) is incorporated into these grandiose job descriptions.

The job descriptions are drawn up by the persons in the jobs to be analyzed. An "analyst" may help in the process. What happens is that

- Your busy people, who see it as an annoying distraction from their work, will throw something together in about an hour, not reflecting that their score for the job will not be set by the normal in-line boss, but by a committee with only a vague idea of what the jobs concerned entail.

- The person with little to do can borrow good books on job evaluation from the library and write a job description to match the best ever recorded. After all, she has the time.

Managers usually put expendable representatives on the analysis team, thus ensuring poor results.

Job Evaluation is nonsensical in its assumption that it is the written description of a job that matters, not what the jobholder actually does.

A quick scan of the job evaluation will show that the writer of a job description can gain handsomely by mastering certain "job evaluation" techniques, as follows:

- Use the words *innovate, analyze,* and *concept* frequently.
- Intersperse words such as *evaluate, original, complex situation, specify,* and *design.*
- Occasionally toss in words like *principles, interpretation, policy, supervise,* and *novel.*
- Words and phrases to avoid include *routine, under instructions, to standard, requiring basic knowledge, simple, ordinary, defined, repetitive, patterned, identical.*
- Imply companywide authority or influence. This may entail racking your brain to remember when you had a discussion, however brief, with a manager not in your division. Record this as "providing ex-

pert advice to managers outside the division on the policy to be followed." The evaluating committee will be dazzled. Your immediate supervisor would probably know that your "advice" was limited to helping that manager come up with a lineup for the company softball team.

- Write from the "top down," as if you were the boss! You may be only a production assistant, but you can say that your work has a direct bearing on the profitability of the entire division and its turnover of $280,000,000!

- Mention the boss as if you were his main source of information.

- If you were ever involved for an hour with an outside firm, give it a page!

The tables used in evaluating jobs look very scientific. One page might typically be headed *Thinking Complexity*, with vertical columns showing "level of thinking," which will range from "thinking within explicit parameters" to "thinking within diversified policies and principles." A horizontal row will show "type of problems solved," varying from "single choice only" to "pathfinding situations involving new concepts." The highest scores are bottom right and the poorest scores are in the top left corner. So if you get points just for hitting on the right terms, knowing those terms can help give you the results you want. The most imaginatively misleading script wins.

I have seen three identical jobs evaluated: One was placed three levels higher in the pay scale than the lowest of the three and two levels higher than the second. Imagine the damage done! Ironically, the most capable person of the three scored lowest because she was extremely busy innovating and meeting deadlines.

Job Evaluation assumes that all people will perform equally in any given job, that it's the position that performs, not the person. By this kind of reasoning, Abraham Lincoln could not be said to have had any special attributes or abilities. It was just the job that had importance.

A typical epidemic of this disease hits the top management level of a firm and spreads downward—on the assumption that you must define the senior jobs before attempting to define the lower positions. That sounds logical but look what happens. Assume a firm has an existing layer reporting to the president, comprised of, say, five vice presidents. If these five jobs are analyzed and given scores which differ in any way, the holders of these posts will appeal the scores until all are equal.

Either the five vice presidents should have agreed in advance to abide by the outcome without appeal, or the whole exercise should not have been undertaken.

Let's say the results read

V.P. Engineering	1244
V.P. Sales	1314
V.P. Finance	1199
V.P. Personnel	1012
V.P. Research & Development	1086

Where do you draw a line to divide them?

You could have two top jobs, or three, or four, or even three levels. Indeed, it is an arbitrary decision of little practical value. You know in advance that you should pay the sales manager more than the personnel manager, but job evaluation makes it easy to avoid the problem.

Having made a mess of the top level—or shelved the application, thus backing off and making a joke of the whole scheme—imagine applying the scheme to the next level down. Here you have 17 jobs, all to be scored on some such basis as:

- Effect of post on success of company

- Number of persons reporting to this post

- Total annual cash flow of the division

All with a matrix grid of scores to be chosen.

When the answers come out, the same difficulty arises—where do you draw lines of seniority (and thus of pay)? Two or three levels must result; otherwise why do the evaluation at all. To leave all 17 on the same level would make a joke of the scheme.

When the lines of demarcation are drawn, everyone just below a line raises an objection and appeals the score. Some of them may be given a higher score by the analysts to prove that all appeals are fairly considered.

The Job Evaluation disease may hit an isolated section of a firm, perhaps all clerical workers, and cause a magic 25 percent upgrading of the category. When this happens, all the other groups feel aggrieved and will join a scheme to be upgraded proportionately.

After a year or two the disease dies away; you are left with a considerably higher payroll. About one-tenth of the time and activity of your employees has been utilized in worrying and talking about the scheme, not to mention the large groups involved as "evaluation committees" who do nothing else for the whole period.

Management by Objective

Here, each manager or supervisor agrees with each person reporting to him or her on what shall be achieved in the next six months. After the six months, a review of progress is held. All sounds very sensible.

What happens? The top-class performer throws out all the targets that were set, because a few weeks into the six month period she will have altered them to get better effect on the success of the firm. The best people are constrained, limited, and bored by stupid targets.

The poor performer will not produce results, even when the objectives are set. All the effort is a waste of the boss's time, which would be better utilized trying to replace the nonperformer with someone better.

The shrewd person rewords and agrees with the boss to things that are already achieved—or almost so. Thus by doing nothing other than normal work the results look great at the end of the prescribed six months.

Consider then how the nonsense is compounded when the management person assessing the subordinates is a second-rate performer!

Attitude Surveys

An internal attitude survey of any given company will show that

- The bosses think it is a good firm that picks people on merit.
- The older folk who have been passed over will say the opposite.
- The young recruits will show a degree of optimism.

The whole thing is like asking someone "Are you comfortable in this room?" The very process of asking the question prejudices them by calling their attention to potential annoyances, like temperature, noise, or color scheme.

Parasitic Units

Don't allow parasitic units to take hold in your firm. They will spend money, grow fat, and cause problems. For example

- Organization review groups will keep messing around with the organization, causing disruption (see above).
- Socioeconomic sections will produce voluminous reports of little value, for example, on the impact of something or other on the environment of New Jersey.
- Human resources deployment divisions will keep interfering with every change of personnel in the firm.

All will grow to at least six or eight persons in pure Parkinson style. After all, the leader of each group can't be expected to do any work.

Such groups will often convene meetings to discuss vague topics, thus wasting the time of others that have work to do. Any section set up that has no direct job to do other than advise and stimulate — or block — will cause huge problems.

The jargon of such a group becomes pervasive. They publish a "news sheet" full of unintelligible nonsense and circulate it around the company.

Have you ever heard this sort of argument: This company is at a watershed. It must have a new look at its corporate identity. Therefore we have commissioned consultants to examine our:

- Color scheme on vans and trucks
- Uniforms for our salespersons
- Company image

These consultants advise that

- Purple is not the "in" color — either on transport or clothing. The new dynamic image needed demands a forward-looking color of the computer age — cerise.
- New advertisements should be run using pieces of poetry (by very obscure poets, whose verse is close to meaningless).

Did you not know that if you have B.O., you should have a good shower? Putting on fine clothes will not obscure the smell!

Justification for a parasitic unit will probably show diagrams of different parts of your organization with arrows pointing in several directions connecting circles of activity. What nonsense!

Productivity Agreements

This "disease" also looks innocent and even attractive. Why not measure the output of workers and then share the spoils of any extra output achieved.

But there are snags:

- When measuring existing output, the workers will go slow so that they can subsequently gain, when they are evaluated.
- Workers who think and plan cannot be measured and will gain in proportion to the gains of the work force that report to them. Therefore, the planners will not object when low standards are assumed as the basis of productivity measurement.

You now set about paying all your work force more for doing the kind of day's work they should have been doing in the first place.

Some poor managers like to hear about productivity agreements. This is because they can sit back waiting for the so-called agreement to be worked out. This may take a year or three, while the bad manager muddles along letting output drift even lower.

When the productivity agreement is struck, with the lousy outputs taken as the normal base, the same poor manager will fail to get a reasonable return for the extra monies paid out—because of continued poor management which will allow liberal interpretation of the deal.

Transaction Review

This exercise is to identify all jobs in the company, say what they are for, and rank them in order of importance. That sounds sensible.

Those listed at the bottom of the 450 jobs should be done away with. This will save money, time, offices, and phone bills. But the reality is different.

One firm quoted by the proponents of this scheme tells me that the 8 percent reduction in staff realized would have happened in any case.

The greater the bluff by a manager, the more protected she will be from this investigation. "That job saves $3,000,000 a year by doing so-and-so" puts that job high up on the list. The exercise gives a reprieve to nonjobs that should be bumped, while the investigation goes on for a year or more.

The study is given an air of scientific accuracy by involving everyone in the exercise. All persons fill up a description of their basic jobs to be analyzed by a team of more senior people.

In the final study by top management all those studies are upended by putting the jobs in their proper order, by ignoring all the fiction written in the job descriptions.

One advantage of all this nonsense is that "everyone participated" in reaching the result—so who can reasonably object?

The Basic Flaw

There is one basic flaw in all the organizational diseases:

- Decentralization
- Centralization
- Job evaluation

- Management by objective
- Annual performance review

They all imply that once effected, the performance of the firm will be far better. All of them assume that the organizational innovation is what matters, not the individual people in their various jobs. Wrong.

Less Serious Diseases

Buzz Words

What about minor diseases that spread in firms? Take buzz words. If the president suddenly is talking about "extrapreneurialism," then everyone catches on to it and begins using it in reports and talks. The employees are like kids using the latest slang words. And, like kids, everyone must drop that piece of jargon when the president introduces a new word or phrase. Otherwise they appear out of date. You will see this disease spread in a wave from corporate headquarters across the world to the smallest outpost of an international firm.

You've heard about "lateral thinking." Right? What is it? It seems to be applied to any crazy idea thrown up—or any good one. It implies that you were stupid not to have applied the technique previously. Next time the term is used, ask what it means, and don't be fobbed off with generalizations.

Vague Inactivity

Statements of intent do not make things happen. For example, those who most vociferously advocate delegation are too often the least likely to do it. Nor do the words "very briefly" work by themselves to prevent a long-winded discourse.

Documents and lectures mention beautifully vague things, such as

- Implementation workload
- Leading-edge tools
- Runaway benefits
- Cost effective service
- Policy review
- Structured programming
- Sophisticated development environment

All such jargon is the bluff that obscures inactivity.

Creative accountancy is a form of vague inactivity in that it can cloud over impending problems. There is great pressure on managers to show better and better results. So dangerous practices can evolve.

If a U.S. bank wants to show better quarterly results, while at the same time it is failing to get payments of interest from a foreign country that has huge debt problems, what can it do? Take a look. It may actually lend the money to the foreign country to enable it to make the interest payments, so that the bank's profits continue to grow! The U.S. bank would not be allowed to include interest payments that were over three months due, so it has to do some "creative" accounting.

Conjuring

Watch for the person with the hoary old plan. It is something unfinished. Anything completed is lacking mystery. It is as if the unfinished state promises great results, implies great strategies laid, and difficulties ahead that will be glorious in the overcoming. There will be always a reason for not completing the task:

- A further budget allocation is needed.
- It awaits the promised reorganization.
- Some eight people are needed to forward this study.

But when completed, is it all just a puff of smoke?

People who do not innovate routinely hang on to one pet idea for years, in terror of completing the task and having nothing further to pursue. At every meeting of the section, at every meeting with management, the hoary plan is dusted off, as if never before mentioned. Why don't they get on with it—or bury it forever?

Some people need a morale boost now and then. So they contrive one. Unable to bring themselves to perform some honest work to get it, they apply for a post in another firm. They imply secretively that they were offered it, but having considered it carefully, declined. Indeed, they should not have applied in the first place unless prepared to move. It's when one such yarn becomes a series of them that the sad truth emerges.

Some salespersons have a similar tendency about the big sale that is just about to be wrapped up. There's always that same hopeful story. They forget you've already heard it three times now.

Do not think that colleagues do not notice and snigger. Saying you are going to do something—or worse still, writing to say you are going to do it—merely proves the opposite. You are rationalizing not doing it. You invite opposition. You want to be able to say "I wanted to do so-and-so but was prevented." But you don't want to take the responsibility of doing it and risking failure.

If you are really intent on doing something, you will just do it—without any announcements.

Some people make their work secret. Nobody is allowed to see or know what goes on. They don't show any correspondence to anyone. They act as if they are the experts and merely ask questions of others without explaining why.

This leads to all sorts of confusion, delay, and messing. They synopsize a technical note and get it wrong. A year later this loses the firm a million dollars.

Conjurers who try to create an impression of dynamism are a menace. An example is the civil servant who after three years of deliberation, issues a statement that "urgent positive action is needed."

Cardinal rules of Chapter 5

DO	DON'T
Be FAIR, FIRM, and FAST	Be VAIN, VAGUE, or VACILLATING
Help your colleagues	Be critical of colleagues
Leave an escape for a worker with whose performance you are dissatisfied	Try too hard to keep your image untarnished
Generate a few friends who will objectively help you	Bother with territorial disputes
Eliminate any post no longer required	Have in-line assistants
Have 6 to 10 reporting to each boss	Have specialists with no set problems and deadlines
Get standards set for everything	Promote anyone just to keep a group happy
Promote staff who are good with people	Overdo reorganizations
	Blame unions or shop stewards for all your woes
	Let management diseases hit your company

6

The Boss

Who Is the Boss

By and large, the most capable people rise to the senior positions in companies around the world. By and large, the boss is the most capable person available at the time of choosing.

Choosing Your Boss

If you are still young, while you are still young, get working for a boss who has quality. Don't stay with someone whom you feel to be incompetent. You will spend far too much time making allowances for ineptitude, checking on what the boss does, following up useless queries, and feeling superior. You are a member of a losing team. Get away horizontally, if necessary.

Move away from a domineering boss. Otherwise you will never learn how to make decisions. It may be a shock to your system to move and suddenly to have to decide things on your own. But don't work for a bully.

Nor should you continue to work for a boss who is unhelpful. You will learn nothing. You will have to act as if she did not exist. You cannot approach her with a problem in its half-warmed condition to pick her brain. Get working for a boss who makes you stretch and imparts knowledge to you, tries you out and loads you up with worthwhile work. You have but one youth to live and you must learn as thoroughly and efficiently as you can.

Communication with the Boss

The most able, intelligent, and effective bosses I have observed are rarely rude—they don't need to be.

Communicate upwards properly. Keep your boss in the picture on what she should know and no more (1 percent of what you are at should about do it). A good manager has this gift. Why? Because he communicates only those items likely to impact directly on the boss.

No boss likes surprises. If your boss is always dashing around and is hard to catch to discuss your job, write brief notes that she can read as she runs. In this way, your progress and failures are constantly in full view, so there are no surprises.

You can only lose in a showdown with your boss. Business hierarchies support themselves from the top. So, except in extreme cases, a supervisor must give support to the next person down the chain of command. Your boss's boss must support her—even if you are right. So hold your temper and bide your time.

In any boss-subordinate situation, the subordinate has to put up with a certain amount of "put down" by the boss. It is the task of the boss to move ahead by reaching decisions rapidly. The skill of the boss is displayed by how well this is effected without insulting or irritating subordinates.

If you have a strenuous disagreement or even a row with your boss, keep it strictly private. Tell nobody, because you might appear to be trying to make a fool of him in public. The ultimate indiscretion would be to inform your boss that he was an idiot and a buccaneer in the presence of some of his colleagues! It happens! And with strange results—or perhaps not so strange. You would need great talent to survive such an event, because some other manager would need to rescue you. It would have to be someone who needed your services badly enough to cope with your erstwhile boss's antipathy in the future.

Some people have a way of making things awkward for the boss. They have a talent for making simple problems difficult to execute: "Are you instructing me to...?" Or they cast things in the worst possible light:

> "Of course we will carry out your instructions, but this will cost an extra $20,000."

> "We can hold those seminars...but if we do we must delay the organizational changes you want."

Try always to terminate any discussion with your boss before he does. In this way you won't need to "be dismissed" and you will not obviously waste his time or take up too large a slice of it. It may sound impressive to say you were no less than two hours with old T. J., but how does old T. J. feel about it? Probably that you are trying to impress him with the complexity of your job—only a small part of his picture—and that you are unfit to run your part of the show.

Pull Your Own Weight

Alter on the spot anything sent back for unimportant alterations by your boss. Have it back in 15 minutes or trivial alterations will appear to possess greater significance. The speed of turnaround will indicate the irrelevance of the change and prevent the irrelevance from irritating you.

Bosses need help from their team every day of every week. The good subordinate never lets the team down with shoddy work, late assignments, or inaccurate calculations.

If something is wrong and you know it, set it right and see that your boss knows it. It is no excuse that someone between you and the boss wants a quiet life. "Oh yes," she will say, "Bert said something about that to me and I was expecting the facts from him, but since he dropped it, I took it that he was satisfied everything was okay." Remember that when the bubble bursts, you may be the one who'll carry the blame. Don't give up when you are dead right (when your esteemed colleagues agree you're right). This exercise can be termed "putting manners on the boss." She'll respect the subordinate who holds his ground and produces facts to enable the company to change course when off beam.

Have some sympathy for your boss. After all, don't you aspire to a job of similar responsibility soon? Faraway hills are green, so make some reasonable allowances for his shortcomings. Maybe you could have a boss who would be far worse.

In Praise of Bosses

You are very conscious of any praise or blame dished out by your boss, aren't you? There are a multitude of theories as to how the boss should go about this. But did it ever strike you that you should praise your boss?

If you are the boss, you know when you do a good piece of work. Wouldn't it be pleasant if a subordinate or two told you that they noticed or appreciated?

It's easy to be critical of a boss, but not so easy to admit when the boss has done something admirable, clever, innovative, or courageous. Why not say so if it's true—face to face?

You grumble that your boss never notices—or certainly never tells you—when you do a good job. It's a bit like making friends. Those who grumble that they have no friends seldom try to make any—they sit around expecting people to call or come by. So if you praise your boss when a particularly good result is evident, that boss is more likely to reciprocate. There may be some people who would disparage such a "mutual admiration" game, but it makes for good teamwork. Remember the song with the lyrics "Accentuate the positive, eliminate the negative"? Give it a try.

Some bosses may feel a bit insecure, particularly if they are new in the job or not very experienced in the technology of the firm. So give a hand; swallow your pride and say "well done."

If you can't get done what should be done, but it is approved further up the line, your influence and effort will be seen as poor by your subordinates. Let your boss think your bright ideas are her own—if she is the type who operates thus—but make sure she is the only one who thinks this is so.

Bosses: The Good, the Bad, and the Ugly

Good supervisors may be affectionately referred to by subordinates as "the boss." Despised bosses are denied such affection and become faceless ciphers.

Would you take it to heart if your boss severely rebuked you? This is a good test of a good boss. If your boss is the peevish or bad-tempered sort, a rebuke will not worry you. More than likely, it will have become standard operating procedure, a regular and expected part of your day. But if your boss is fair, honest, composed, helpful, and able, then you should and would take it to heart if such a reprimand were forthcoming.

The boss is often accused of changing his style of management. But of course this will and must happen. In good times the conditions of employment will improve and the boss will appear friendly, generous, and broad-minded. In bad times people may be let go; conditions will worsen. The boss (the same one) now becomes miserly, mean, and narrow-minded.

When the boss does something that is daft, turns out to be a loser, and costs the firm losses, what do you say? Remember that every boss has to take risks and try to change things for the better. So now and then there will be a debacle. Would you advocate that a boss do nothing—just let things roll along as they are?

Judge such episodes together with all the other efforts by that boss. If the general trend is for a more efficient, innovative, thriving business, do not nag about the one blooper. It is dangerous to become fixated on one loss-making effort. Some subordinates can think and talk about nothing but the one pass the boss dropped—forgetting all the scores achieved.

If you have an intelligent boss who is fair-minded and not vindictive, then you act likewise. Remember, it takes two to make war. Someone has decided that the boss is the right person for the job—and it wasn't you!

Some expect that the boss should "love" them, for example, by frequent and public statements on the quality and quantity of their work. This is just another form of inferiority complex. The boss should not love or hate any subordinate—just know how to get the best from them all the time.

Each subordinate needs different treatment. Flattery works for some; a businesslike approach is appreciated by others; a supportive helping hand is needed by some; others like maximum independence of action with measurement of results as the sole criterion for success. So the boss has to be cunning, devious, or charming—depending on the circumstances—and on the point of view!

The boss who calls for "open and frank" discussions with subordinates may really be saying

"I want you to confess your sins to me."

"I fear that you are not keeping me informed of impending doom."

"You must be 'open and frank,' but I'll be damned if I'll let you in on my plans and ideas, not even the ones that might unseat you from your job!"

What of the president who read about the success of the "open, participative style of management," thought it a great idea, and issued a directive that in future it was to apply throughout the company—with no exception and without argument! He did not see the irony.

There is an almost irresistible temptation to be rude and, indeed, insulting, if you are a boss. Nobody can contradict you. At long last, after all the years of putting up with rude bosses, you have arrived. In a meeting with immediate subordinates, you can insult any one without fear of retaliation, because if they are rude in return, you have an excuse for removing them from their post.

Many excuses are put forward for such rude behavior:

"I am too busy to be polite."

"I shoot from the hip; there's nothing devious about me."

"My managers like it that way."

In fact, it is an ego trip. To quote the Irish parliamentarian Edmund Burke, "The greater the power, the more dangerous the abuse."

The same boss, putting forward the same complaints directly one-to-one, in private, will get back the full answers and denials and proofs, and may have to back off and agree that the subordinate has in fact done a good job. The boss's ego gets no joy from this. Sometimes such a boss will write accusations to a subordinate. This can be so that he can prove at a later date that he tackled the problem in time.

Some bosses see nothing right in their own company. They see nothing wrong in competitors' firms. Why?

- They accept bragging by competitors as fact.
- They see as exaggeration and bragging any excellence in their own firm.

Imagine what this does for morale.

A boss who acts as if all subordinates were the enemy needs redeeming features galore. This is the boss who

- Keeps changing direction
- Issues salvoes highly critical and insulting
- Is irritable
- Talks of "turning on" the work force
- Thinks that "constant change" keeps everyone "on their toes"
- Thinks that uncertainty breeds success

Walking the Tightrope

If you want to get your boss to change, how do you succeed? It very much depends on what sort of boss you've got. I remember a note I once received from a manager reporting to me. This person rarely resorted to such means as writing. He was a doer, not a writer.

So when I read "Your memo of the 9th instant has surprised, saddened, and somewhat disappointed me," he had my undivided attention!

Chastising your boss is a delicate exercise. You could easily end up in an antagonistic, counterproductive relationship. One possible way to move your boss to change is to try to introduce some humor into the situation. In Ireland we are rather renowned for our limericks. Composing a limerick would be one way, but the range of ways to bring humor to a sensitive situation is very broad. Use your imagination.

Never let any of your colleagues know that you and your boss are engaged in any such minuet, if only because any one of them might derive some perverse pleasure from reporting it to the office gossip. Such matters may take on personal overtones and should be dealt with discreetly. Also, such incidents should be held to a minimum, infrequent, temporary, and private in the dealings between a good boss and employee. So choose your battles wisely.

The Big Boss

The direction a company takes is decided by the president. All the information in the world cannot be substituted for sound judgment, wisdom, and foresight. The decisions that will stem from this will not please everyone in the company—only those whose empires will expand. But having decided, plans will be laid to achieve the set aims as quickly as economically possible.

Some sore heads will result—yours may be one of them. When policy changes do not suit you, do not take such occurrences as a personal affront. If you do, and if you adopt an obstructionist stance because of it, you prove yourself unhelpful to a clearly enunciated corporate goal. Either get behind the changes or get out.

The Bicycle Brigade

Parkinson was right about the activities of a board of directors. They will spend an hour discussing a bicycle shed—because they know what it is and can contribute meaningfully to such a project. The same disease goes right down through an organization. Each boss will show the most interest in what she knows most about. This gives the impression that she will not let go of her previous job. Thus, if the production manager becomes general manager, she will tend to give many comments and suggestions on production matters. That general manager will see it as contributing best to the success of the company by using her many years of experience.

Do not entirely underestimate the contribution of the "bicycle shed" brigade. They will contribute in the area in which they have experience—be it economics, engineering, accountancy, building costs, or marketing. But do not criticize because they keep to their area of greatest knowledge and value. They are afraid to comment on the many important aspects of the business (including your specialty) where they are out of their depth.

Cardinal Rules of Chapter 6

DO	DON'T
Pick a good boss	Waste the boss's time
Keep the boss informed	Give up if you are right just because the boss objects
Appreciate an intelligent boss	Stay working for an incompetent
	Be rude if you are a boss
	Be overcritical of your boss

7

Of Carrots and Sticks

Practical Recruitment Guidelines

"You can't make a silk purse out of a sow's ear." This means that you had better recruit good people and promote the best performers. Otherwise you will lose. No amount of organizational theory or staff motivation will help very much. Watch those firms that attract the smartest people—not just by offering dollars. Indeed, look within a large firm and see where the smart people go. That division gives the best performance and will continue to do so. Good people gravitate to where the challenging work goes on. Young recruits will find out which companies and which parts of companies are dynamic. Poor performers will have to accept second best and join poor firms or poor sections in a good firm. Thus the gap widens between the good and bad.

One successful firm had a unique policy of recruitment. They took managers from the upper-middle standard graduating from the universities. The reasoning was that

- These young women and men were intelligent.

- They probably had a good time because they didn't have to kill themselves studying, so they were likely to be good mixers.

- The very top of the class can be risky. They can be marvelous or disastrous, depending on how they attained that level. If it took them studying 10 hours per day, seven days per week that's the disaster. Or they may just be very clever, in which case they're good enough for any job.

- The bottom of the class are probably lazy or not too bright.

129

This policy was pursued with great success.

Pretest fresh college graduates by giving them a project, to discover, before you employ any of them, the kind of work they do. You will learn

- If they can define a problem
- If they can work to a conclusion
- If they can work hard
- If they can get along with people

Don't judge a prospective employee on bulk, hair, or clothing. Young persons who are dressed like you may be doing so just for effect during the interview.

Take on a few people who have been around a bit and have seen first-hand the drab green of those faraway hills. They will help to counteract starry-eyed youngsters easily dazzled by the lure of greener pastures.

Try to fill positions with people who have experience at the lower levels of the same job. For example, when recruiting for a design office, recruit people who have helped put together the things they are supposed to design.

Be careful not to recruit persons who are already being passed over in their existing firms. Let's say you run an advertisement in the papers, something like:

> "Wanted, technicians with three years experience in heating and ventilating equipment."

The three years is a deadly stipulation. That is just the time when their worth is first being tested for promotional posts. You get marvelous résumés and all the duds thrown up in your competitors' offices; they have just been passed over in the first promotion race since they joined that other firm.

If you hire this way, you will appear to have great success in filling your nine openings. But in 10 years time you will have a lump of deadwood in your organization. Such careless recruiting does severe harm to your business. The chances are that one of the nine will become the union representative complaining of lack of promotional opportunities.

Head Hunting

The alternative way of getting those with three years' experience runs like this: You are at a meeting of the Institution of Heating Engineers and meet the manager of a division in another company. "Jean," you say, "I am thinking of offering Tom Brown who works with you a post with us." If Jean replies "Dagnabit, I'll have to give him a raise to stop you!" you know it's a good one—but check whether Jean was fooling by finding out at the interview if Tom really did receive a sudden pay raise.

Take on some people with outside experience not available in the company. This will improve techniques and can save money on consulting fees.

Avoid hyping your firm. Why produce glittering advertisements that the firm has "wonderful opportunities for promotion" unless it is expanding into a new field or with a new product? You are setting yourself up for a load of disgruntled employees—unless, of course, you have a plan to shoot two or three fairly senior managers monthly. Leave it to the applicant to decide—on the facts—whether she wants to join. Advertising "wonderful promotional opportunities" for a middle management position can be mighty insulting to existing staff, who also read the newspapers.

Never overpay to recruit. If money is all you have to offer, the bees will leave the honey as soon as they find a more interesting job.

Do as Napoleon did. Seek out marshals who are lucky. Maybe they make their own luck. Herman the German, the head of General Electric Gas Turbines, had a notice in his office that said "I work so hard I get lucky." And Gary Player said a similar thing: "The more I practice, the luckier I get."

What to Look For

Do not take recruitment or subsequent promotion selections lightly. The greatest single asset a company can have is people who are better than the competitors' people. This matters more than the organizational setup, the amount of delegation, centralization or decentralization, or most other aspects of management.

Whenever you're recruiting, it can't hurt to ask yourself the following question: If you were going into the jungle, which of the candidates would you most want to bring with you?

Always be looking for employees with good judgment. It is rare, and does not come in easily recognizable packages. If someone's work is always right, cherish that person. Such results come from outstandingly good judgment, not just good luck. A particularly good test would be the number of times you have opposed this employee, and then found him or her to be right. Employees with good judgment are not sycophants. They are helping the company to reach better decisions.

Look for the one who always emerges from the pack with the ball.

Others are holding jerseys, hacking shins, facing the wrong way, shouting for a pass. It's a sense of positioning and timing—and keeping an eye on the ball. It's also a spark of genius. You can't educate or train anyone to gain the spark of genius of a Pele or a Muhammed Ali, any more than an Einstein or an Eisenhower.

There are some who excel once tasks are set down for them. Slightly better performers begin to set their own tasks once they are put through the exercise a few times. The best of all are those who set their own proper tasks right from the start.

There are two extremes of quality:

- Streams of action, hard work, decisions, and no talk

- Lots of talk and meetings and committees and questions and more talk, but not a single decision emerging and little actual work

You play a game of golf with a stranger. The stranger hits a perfect shot. "Show me that club," you say. But did it ever strike you that it is the skill of the player that counts? I once played a round of golf with a man who had no clubs or golf shoes. He used whichever club each of us in the group said we could not manage—my driver, someone else's three iron, another person's putter—and he went around Ireland's most difficult course in less than par! Remember that the same applies at work. It is not the computer but the person using it that solves the problem. It is not the pen that composes the poetry!

Shakespeare's Julius Caesar understood the principle only too well. If "yon Cassius has a lean and hungry look," get him—unless, of course, you are afraid to get good subordinates, lest they oust you.

Promotion Guidelines

Compatibility is one thing, but guard against a tendency to select people just because they share your style or temperament. Often, the interaction of two different temperaments will benefit both parties. To avoid creating a one-sided situation, use formal assessments as a yardstick for choices.

If you pick a weak person for promotion

- For the sake of keeping the peace

- Because he or she is "in line" for it

- Because the person happens to be in your own section

- To foster hope in the area from which the project is drawn

- Because you can't promote too many from one group and must thus take the best from another
- Because he knows every nut and bolt of every machine in the plant (this is a favorite rationalization—"this candidate will be useful faster.")

you may be forging a weak link into your chain. Do you have the time to

- Force weak managers to keep up pace
- Hope the weakling's subordinates will keep the ship afloat
- Do the work yourself

Sometimes it's better not to fill a job at all.

If you have an organization where intelligent, able people are bottled up by dullards and bluffers, you will have an unhappy company with poor output. And it should be no surprise that the good people will leave first chance. The bozos will always be around. They have nothing to lose and everything to gain. But then, of course, this all assumes that the general manager possesses top-notch qualifications. If not, you had better get out yourself. Of course, if you are a dullard and bluffer too, you won't see any of this going on and it won't matter.

Promote nine out of ten on merit and leave the tenth opening to allow for older employees reaching their peak. If you don't, the low flyers will see no chance of reaching a peak and you will break their spirit. Every organization should give consideration to achieving a reasonable distribution of employees by age and ability.

There is nothing wrong with being in a middle-level job, being excellent at it, and never moving higher. The genius in selection is to have each person stop at a point where he or she is on top of the job—no higher, no lower.

Who to Promote

Selection of people for promotion is mighty important to you in your job and to how you yourself will be able to perform.

Promote on results—there is no substitute—even if you don't particularly like the person or if you never meet socially. If someone is clearly identifiable as the one who produces the goods, up she goes. For example, a person who moves into a division where losses are piling up and turns it around is obviously someone of value. You might consider grooming that manager for your biggest or most difficult division.

Henry Ford once said of Lee Iacocca, "There are some people you just don't like." What a mistake. You don't have to like a performer.

Personal characteristics, however irksome—flamboyant style, loud voice, affectation, fast car, right- or left-wing views—are not a sound basis for rejecting someone. The most capable people require more handling, because they have more imaginative and useful ideas.

Promote the person who shows signs of ability or qualities that will be more prominent in the higher position. The "Peter Principle" may apply if you make your fastest or most productive technician a supervisor, but not if you make into a supervisor the good technician who is deft at handling staff and planning work.

An employee who can initiate and instigate has potential. He could even be instigating things that are supposed to be in his boss's province. Promote the person who has the kind of ideas that will move the job forward a decade and who can prove it to you with concrete results, facts and figures, dollars and cents.

Promote mental heavyweights. Lightweights get blown about with every stiff breeze (and some that are not so stiff). This assumes you don't want to run a one-person show and surround yourself with sycophants.

Heavyweights

- Are always on time
- Do not make excuses
- Do not let *you* delay
- Look like potentials to take on your job
- Are right in practice—even when you had grave doubts
- Are very impatient

"Impatient?" you ask. Of course, impatience can be of value to a manager—used in moderation—and it is a common trait among heavyweights. Here's an old ditty to serve as a reminder of just how impatience can be an aid to management:

Impatience is a virtue,

Obtain it if you can,

It gets you working faster,

And gives you the upper hand.

Don't promote people solely in the hope that they will grow into the job. Nor should you promote on the argument that an employee was "not bad" in a position and that a change may bring out that person's best qualities. A loser is likely always to remain a loser. Don't take chances on someone who has been truly tried out in a position of responsibility and has failed.

Whenever I have allowed myself to be talked into breaking this rule, the results have been disastrous. Don't listen to arguments like, "I think he would be better at design work." This means he is hopeless at whatever he is now doing and will be hopeless at anything else.

Beware the applicant with the longest résumé. Quite the most useless performers are able to fill 20 pages when applying for a promotion. It displays a lack of balance and sensitivity. In a way, it's an insult to the interviewer.

Make a rule that anyone promoted must move within three weeks (don't say a month—it's too vague) or you must be told why, with the donor department and the receiving department agreeing on the reason for the delay. After all, the person promoted could break a leg or leave the firm with a month's notice, and then the donor department would have to get along a person short.

The Chaff

In selecting for promotion watch for danger signs in the make-up of the contenders:

- The person who talks nonstop, never listening to anyone else. This type thinks she learned it all before you had the luck to acquire her.

- Anyone who can't deal with alcohol or drugs—on or off the job—is dangerous.

- The one who follows you into more than one club. It may be coincidence, but consider carefully. It may not be.

- Persons who have no (or a poor) sense of humor. Dour or melancholy personalities seem to work like magnets. They attract similar types around them and lump into groups that are either hurt, offended, or angered by everything.

When promoting, watch out for people who are overly deferential. Why are they like this? Is it because they are impressed with you personally? (Goodness knows, why should they be?) Or perhaps they are impressed with the furniture and fittings in your office, or the prestige of your post. Sycophants are two-faced; they flatter the boss, then turn around and harass the snake hooey out of subordinates.

If anyone is impressed by a job, then that person clearly is not able for it. Awe is hardly a quality that keeps organizations moving. Able persons need the position in order to make sorely needed improvements to what in their view is an unimpressive job (as presently performed).

Avoid putting a "kingfisher" into a planning job. The kingfisher is a bird that allows no other competing bird on its stretch of river. Get managers who are not afraid to consider all the pros and cons—even if they have to forfeit a little power by the result. Otherwise your forward planning will consist of justification of past practices (as handled by the kingfisher) and demarcation disputes with other departments. People who demarcate are not able for the job, cause trouble, and make unnecessary wage claims.

Study your subordinates to see if any of them like the job they are doing so much that they isolate it from the scrutiny of top management. You may find they are not really able to cope with the job they have, let alone take on something more difficult further up the line.

Most offputting is the person who is often right, but whose judgment is eccentric. It's sad, but such a trait never seems to get cured.

Avoid those with "read-only" memory; that is, those who can't take in any new information, but can only give fixed opinions that never change.

Looking through the back windshield of a car shows you all that has happened. It is easy to be critical of the driver, telling her what wildlife or road debris she has run over. Some people are very good at criticizing what others have or have not done, but such people are not leaders or innovators. They are useful, but they are what might be termed negative people.

The useful people are the drivers—those who choose the route, avoid the potholes, keep an eye out for oncoming or cross traffic, and watch for falling trees or rocks. These are the positive people who improve the performance of a firm.

The person who is perpetually making a case for higher pay—without his direct boss making that case—is a nuisance. Examine his job and how he is performing and you will very likely find the quality of his work is nothing to shout about. He spends his time arguing about salary instead of doing an excellent job and applying for promotion through proper channels. Get right to the source of this problem. Go through the job, step by step. Take a maintenance electrical supervisor, for example. Check to see that every single item of electrical gear is 100 percent operable. The quality of the maintenance will be in inverse proportion to the number of claims for higher pay.

More Mileage Out of Your Interviews

It is easier and more economic of your time to interview all the contend-
than to explain afterwards to all the losers why they did not get the job.

Interviewing for a job has another advantage. The losers can go
home to their spouses and say "If not for that #!*&* Reilly, I'd be
okay—do you know what he asked me? Obviously he is prejudiced
against me because that question had nothing whatever to do with running a computer software office." The winner thinks Reilly very fair
and perspicacious.

Always make your questions specific and brief, and get quantification
or verification for everything possible:

"Did you publish it? Can I read a copy?"

"What date was the project completed? What was the planned date?"

As the interviewer, you don't need to talk for more than 5 percent of
the interview. Are you one of those people who monopolizes the interview time expounding on the history of the company, the division's annual goals, or the person who held the position before? What are you trying
to prove—how smart you are? Heaven help the unfortunate interviewee, or
any colleague helping with the interview—probably your boss.

Don't get chatty with the people you interview—about their family,
outside interests, and the like. Some interviews contain little else. If you
hire or promote the person—which, after all, is what you're trying to de-
termine in the interview—you can find all this out at the annual staff party.

Never pick staff for promotion solely on the basis of a 20-minute interview. You'll be fooling yourself. You can't possibly know

- If the prospect is cooperative

- If he or she is productive

- If the interviewee has sound judgment

Use assessments for everyone in the company, and refer to these
when you interview (see the section on Staff Appraisal). Without assessments to back up an interview, it is difficult to pick the best person. It
may mean that the older applicant, or the one with the most years service,
has the better chance for success, and not necessarily the best applicant.

Try not to harbor prejudices that will tip the scale in favor of anyone from outside your own staff. Some managers actually believe this way. This is the "grass-is-greener" syndrome. It's amazing how well-groomed, well-dressed, well-spoken, erudite, and knowledgeable some perfectly useless performers can appear in a short interview.

Use a long interview and prepare precise questions for those who come from outside your company. Make it as thorough as you can. Check with someone in the interviewee's present company if you can. This is worth a day's interviewing. I've seen some ghastly blunders in over- and underestimating the abilities of strangers.

Promises, Promises

Never advise a subordinate to take any particular post. If it doesn't work out, the person may blame it on you and not on herself. You may have seen cases in which an erstwhile colleague was advised to take a job and then fossilized. It's impossible to win every time, but try to be sensitive to this kind of thing.

By the same token, never prematurely promise anything in the way of salary increase, promotion, prospects, fringe benefits, power, or extra responsibilities. This can engender false hope. Make sure you have approval to do so from the person who makes the final decision.

Some managers, in fits of egotism or inflated confidence, stupidly think they can promise something and then present it to the boss as a fait accompli, thus bullying the boss into accepting it. This is a dangerous practice. Even if you are sure, certain, and positive; even if you have in writing that such is normal and acceptable; even if you have trod the same path twenty times before and encountered no problems; still you raise hopes which may have to be dented or dashed. Even if you later fulfill the promise, your word is effectively broken.

It is far better to leave staff with unconfirmed hopes which will give satisfaction when and if they are realized. Avoid the temptation to butter someone up with an early promise. The good feeling gained may give way to remorse when you can't deliver the goods. You are not in the game for personal gratification.

If you ever privately promise someone promotion before the formal interviews take place (to appear to be the only interviewer who really matters), or for the kind of personal gratification mentioned above, word will get out and you will be seen as a manipulator.

Building a Team

Having colleagues and employees who are friendly and cooperative with each other is the greatest guarantee of success in business. How do you get it? Perhaps your predecessor left it to you. It's not the person who laughs most, but the one with humor and integrity, that you want. Integrity can be seen in the one who is able to engage in a healthy amount of self criticism and self evaluation, and in a person who, without jealousy, procrastination, ifs, ands, or buts, considers improvements offered by colleagues and changes immediately.

Work hard to obtain a friendly, helpful, encouraging, stimulating atmosphere. Avoid strenuously a repressive, authoritarian atmosphere.

When staffing up a new plant or office, do not take everyone from the same age group, for example, between 25 and 35. This may work well for five years, but soon the people in lower jobs see that there is little or no prospect of promotion for 20 years. They will be turned off. Taking a cross section of ages gives a balance of maturity to the family and ensures continuity. You may hear Joan (at 55) advising young Joe: "Take it easy, we tried that in 1984 and here is what happened..." Leo, who sees himself filling Joan's job in a few years, listens carefully.

Not all companies are like this in practice, but I've seen it done both ways and believe that a reasonable mix of ages is a good thing. The older people do not necessarily have to fill the most senior jobs. It's just that a scattering of mature people, well used to doing a good day's work, who are cheerful and get on well with others, can have a very beneficial effect on a firm.

Fooey if your personnel department, or anyone else, thinks that it's better to employ people for a full career, who will qualify for a full pension in the company scheme. The person taken on at 50 may be happy to contribute a higher percentage to the pension fund and to get a lower pension at retirement. There are laws about all that, but it is good sense in any case.

Be prepared to bend your organization to suit any real talent you have. Outstanding people are rare, so don't hem them in with too little scope. And be careful not to land yourself in trouble when a good person leaves—or dies. It happens. Don't jump to fill the post unless you have another person who is or can be just as good.

Don't employ only people who have what you see as a 100 percent chance of going all the way to the top. You need people suited to jobs at every level, so don't have university graduates sweeping the floor or trained accountants in pen-pushing clerical posts.

Laugh

It's fun—doing something enjoyable and doing it well is one of the great pleasures in life. It has not gone out of fashion. There is no need to be ashamed or shy about saying that you love working—that you love your work.

There is great pleasure in working with a group that can laugh and joke as they work along.

The most terrifying type of supervisor is the one without a keen sense of humor. And these types are at their very worst when they try to make a joke—because it always falls flat.

The Call to Action

If you want action, try something which will amuse or set people to talking. Try a memo consisting of just a question mark.

$$?$$

Sending a signed and typed letter or memorandum is not a sure recipe for getting the desired action. Did you ever try sending a poem? Yes, a piece of doggerel. It's not necessary to sign it (perhaps best not to). That adds to the amusement. This tactic is very useful when you want action by an outside agency that will not act. Say, for example, the company car park is badly managed and the spaces are only about 60 percent occupied at any one time. (The manager won't fill spaces first come, first served, but leaves open the spaces of people on vacation or out for the day.) Employees are parking their cars a mile away and are very frustrated by this inefficiency on the part of the manager in charge of the car parks. Try a limerick. Issue copies galore. And don't sign it.

A signed memo can be a declaration of war. The recipient has to retaliate, defend, justify, and explain. An unsigned limerick demands no answer. Who would you answer? The author's identity is a bit uncertain. The only answer is to correct the condition that gave rise to the limerick.

I've seen cases where two years of pungent memo warfare got no result, and one piece of sarcastic unsigned doggerel got the desired action within 24 hours. It allows the recipient to save face and enter into the spirit of things. She can prove to be a sport, and maybe pen an even better verse. After all, who wants to be dubbed a bad sport?

Forget It

Any difference of opinion, argument, disappointment, practical joke, sly behavior—forget the lot. If you don't, you will harbor grudges against everyone around you.

It's like a traffic accident. Both parties firmly believe they are in the right. It's a waste of time and effort trying to persuade the other driver the fault was his.

Treating the Troops Right

When you talk to staff who report to the manager reporting directly to you, ask questions, but do not make decisions that override the opinions or decisions of the manager in between. If there is a problem or conflict, wait until you leave the scene and then tackle the manager to see if the controversial line of action can be justified. It's okay to "tease out" details by asking questions: "Did you investigate having three outlets...?"

If you don't adopt this approach, you will have a difficult time obtaining the loyalty of the manager—or you may lose it if you already had it. Your visits will appear to be designed to make an ass of him in front of his own staff.

Ask your subordinates what, in their opinion, you are not doing that you should be doing. Having done so, work on it, thus strengthening your hand to get them to react favorably (undefensively) to similar constructive criticisms that you may offer. Don't argue over any of their comments. That is merely trying to prove you really are perfect. This exercise is particularly useful if you can ask three managers (one of noteworthy independence, one especially competent, and one respected for reliability and outspokenness) to give you in writing their frank comments. If you get nothing worthwhile, it may mean you don't have their trust. And would it surprise you if all three listed the same item first without knowing the other two had also been asked? Such a thing happened to me. It just meant that the item they all called to my attention sure was a first priority for change.

Remember that nobody understands intelligence superior to their own. Consider the number of people you regard as slow-witted and muddled, versus the number you know can outthink you. Then pause and reflect: Are you some kind of divine entity? Obviously not. Realize that superior intelligence cannot be properly appreciated. If it could, you would have it!

Never be sarcastic at subordinates' expense—particularly with anyone else listening. It's a cheap shot, too easy and too hurtful. Think how you'd feel if the roles were reversed.

If you are criticizing the work or performance of a subordinate, keep it private. Under no circumstances do you let other subordinates know. Making a public theatrical spectacle of correcting someone is not an edifying experience.

Do not let any employee damage their health, mental or physical, by

- Overwork
- Unhealthy working conditions

even if they are oblivious to the danger and may oppose any changes.

Never confuse authority lines by asking one person to do a job and then chatting up her assistant or supervisor about getting it done. Nobody knows now who ultimately is responsible for getting it done. And remember, if it's a controversial sort of action anyway, everyone will welcome any excuse to pass the buck. You've given them an out if the project falls behind schedule.

Studiously avoid discussing one of your subordinate managers' matters with other subordinate managers. The word will get back that you are trying to set one against the other and if they are honorable people, they will not express amateur opinions on a colleague's work.

Compensation

See that your staff's pay is right for the job they do. Don't settle for anything less. But don't overpay either.

Don't just act as a bystander, commenting casually on genuine staff pay-related claims as they pass up and down your level in the organization. Make up your mind what is right, take off your coat, and go after it.

If your better performers are paid more (by bonus if necessary), there is more justice and less frustration. You can't allow a system in which poor performers receive the same pay as excellent performers. It will tend to kill initiative.

A simple scheme used in one department of a large multinational corporation was to tie the bonus of each person to the breakdown rate of one piece of the machine. The result was very impressive. Where previously a machine would be stopped, opened up, examined, and then repaired, a new method of peering in without opening up the machine was devised. The breakdown rate tumbled in a matter of months.

Managers who waffle on and on about performance bonus never pay it. They insist that they are "developing a scheme." In reality, they fear distinguishing between the five persons that report directly to them. How can you pay three of them a bonus on performance without interminable arguments with the other two about

- Favoritism
- Reasons why the boss prevented them from performing

So rather than turn off two out of five, nothing is done other than advocate that it must be done.

Result-Getting Tactics

For each person in each post you supervise, whether functional or not, assign specific tasks and get specific dates for completion. The date should be set by the person concerned and agreed to by you.

Always specify the exact date by which you want results. But be fair. If everyone knows you must submit budgets by 16 March, don't ask for them on 16 February from your subordinates. They have to work them out; you only have to check and approve them.

If data requested or the answer to a query is not received by the time you asked for it, do it yourself or have it done by someone else, and let the person who should have done it see the answer. Let everyone know that this is the ruling. But you had better answer everything that reaches you well within the deadline!

When you want a quick, but only approximate, answer, make it clear. "Give me, to the nearest $10,000, by Wednesday the 14th, what you will spend by the end of the year."

This prevents the detail hound from taking up too much time giving you an answer of a total expenditure of $64,267.42, which is of no interest to you when you are trying to ascertain whether total costs will be close to $41,000,000 for the year. It should also prevent follow-up calls or notes amending it to $64,268.31.

Don't accept excuses for lack of results:

"All these people were foisted on me when I took over the job."

"If I could hand-pick my own people, I'd make this place hum."

"I'm no manager. A real manager gets to hire and fire his own staff."

To put it another way, this manager could only captain a football team entirely selected by himself—not by the team manager. This is the "canonization complex." He's the saint and his colleagues and predecessors are the sinners.

The Problem with Putting the Best Face on Things

You must set the precise targets against which managers are to report. Comparing the performance of each management unit with the "average" has drawbacks. In practice, each manager will select for presentation those items on which performance looks good in relation to the average. Indeed, the figures will tend to show everyone better than average on everything!

Some will compare with other branches of the company; others will compare with the total company; others with the national industrial figure. Each can be selective in what is presented. One compares with the company average for overtime; another with the average for officer staff for absenteeism; a third with the regional average for accidents. They will show something at which they excel. No manager will voluntarily show performance worse than average. So check the figures and set the averages against which they are to report.

Showing performance in relation to the rate of inflation, for example, is meaningless. Such comparisons should be banned. The rate of inflation is a concoction of anything and everything and it has little relevance to performance. It allows nothing for

- Increases in productivity
- Increased efficiency
- Elimination of waste
- Better design

If you can't lick the socks off the inflation rate every week and every year, you should be sacked.

Watch out for graphs that do not show the zero line. They start at a portion of the graph that exaggerates and flatters. What looks like a huge improvement may really be a tiny advance, shown by altering the scale used.

Abstruse parameters will be used to try to show a good picture; for example, financing cost per $1000 collected.

Reduction in the "percentage increase per annum" of something horrible is the ultimate nonsensical way to show an improvement. Are we supposed to be heartened to learn that the ship is sinking a little more slowly than usual?

Even where a figure is recorded as worse (after every attempt to massage it into positiveness), an excellent reason will be given—a storm or earthquake or influenza epidemic:

"It was out of our hands."

"We would've realized unprecedented growth, but..."

Well...okay...fine.

The only presentation that may show figures worse than average will be from a new manager, who can still write it off to the failings of her predecessor. She'll learn all the tricks by next year.

Setting Goals

Challenge managers to produce in writing the main improvements which they think must be undertaken—only those worth 1 percent of the turnover of their department are worthwhile. If no suggestions come forth, then the manager is no good. The most convincing suggestions are the ones that advocate a reduction of control over resources by the manager concerned, because she must end up with less staff or expenditure. You, as a manager yourself, must come up with better items than any of your subordinates. That is what you are there for, or else someone blundered by putting you in charge.

Help subordinates to reach their goals. Ask if you can help in any way. But the goal is still theirs, and the credit. If you want any improvement or alteration in their work, be specific and give the exact reasons.

Vague aims are no use. Everything that looks specific is not necessarily: "We will increase efficiency by 2 percent." That looks very precise, but what is "efficiency?" And how do you measure 2 percent of it?

Ask for a detailed plan for achieving a specific improvement. Probe. Ask questions. "What capital investment is needed?" "Is it an economic proposition?"

Staff Appraisal

Make a formal appraisal of staff yearly (or every two or three years for more senior staff). If anyone is scored below the acceptable level in any one area, find out by discussion with that person

- How she rates herself.
- Where the discrepancy (if any) is when compared with the official result; often there is none. Where there is a discrepancy, a useful discussion will ensue, because that is where the candidate has an exaggerated idea of his abilities.
- Reasons for the discrepancy.

It is death to a company if the bluffers, the lazy, the chancers begin to float to the top because top managers do not know the score. Install an upside down assessment scheme to allow junior managers to assess their seniors. As a senior manager yourself, listen carefully to individual workers to find out the score on other managers.

Don't show assessments to staff concerned, or the managers assessing them will underplay their ratings. A young person who knows she's been rated highly could get a swollen head and be ruined. Be happy to promote her and hope she keeps it up. However, let staff know if they are rated below the acceptable level on any one aspect of their job, and give them the chance to discuss it and improve.

Design an assessment form for each specific job category. Don't use the same one for the whole company, say, to cover both salespeople and research chemists. It would have to be so general that it would be useless.

Use more than three categories of performance. Having just "Poor," "Average," and "Excellent" means that most people will be placed in the middle grade. This won't tell you much. Still, make every effort to have a simple form and a simple guide to scores.

You can judge how good managers are at sizing up their staff by the assessments they submit. One may grade all subordinates as "excellent." Another may grade everyone as "bad." This should clue you in that they are deficient in the judgment category themselves. Seldom will an entire group of people fall too far short of a roughly bell-shaped curve when evaluated.

Advise those who perform poorly in a given area that they are in a job requiring good performance in that area, and to look around for a move within or without the company.

Assessments by two separate managers who have been the boss of an individual will not necessarily concur, but they should present a clearer picture. It should at least show if a person is in the wrong job, is okay for the job, or is shaping up to be outstanding or poor. Over a few years, the assessments will clearly show the good performers and the poor ones and ensure that no bluffers and incompetents get ahead. I can vouch for the usefulness from practical experience.

Probation

If you have occasion to question the performance of an employee, call for the file and you will often see that when this employee was first taken on, there were doubts—extended probation, poor attendance, lack of attention to the job—followed by hopes and hopes and more hopes.

Better to have let such people go in the beginning, during their probationary period, before they make a career of being no use. If your company doesn't have an initial probation period, it might be useful to institute it.

Spotting the Losers

If a manager makes one serious error of judgment, issue a warning. If he makes three, withdraw from him authority on matters of serious import. If you are managing effectively, not more than 1 percent of your staff should need such treatment.

Remember, it's only those who are regularly late arriving in the morning who will object to a check on timekeeping. They'll probably stress the obvious truth that, in their job, performance can't be measured by minutes spent in the office. But the example to junior staff engaged on routine work can be disastrous.

Watch carefully those who continually claim that they are "busy." If anyone claims to always be 100 percent occupied, he should not get any further. Correction...he should probably not be in his present job. His "busyness" means that he has no time to improve the job, or to make a case for, and battle to get, improvements.

If all those claiming to be "overloaded" would just shut up moaning about it for a month, think of the vacuum that would be formed, a vacuum that could be filled with useful work. Think of the increased productivity!

Variations on the Theme of Incompetence

Those who are not able to do their job just do not do it. They turn back and

- Write reports
- Draw up plans
- Call meetings of colleagues to get their imprimatur for these documents (this will be a tedious process)
- Hire consultants to say what should be done
- Submit proposals for new organization—so radical that there is little chance of acceptance
- Complain bitterly about the lack of service from other parts of the organization

There is an inverse correlation between complaints about the amount of work to be done, or about lack of promotions, and the capability of the complainer to do it.

It's a pleasure to work with managers who dig in without continual reference to

- Work load
- Staff shortage
- Idle assistants

You know you'll get from them the right answer to any query in short order. It's no such pleasure to deal with the clown who has the most intricate and complex reasons for doing nothing:

"The insurance aspects of night travel in the USSR prohibit..."

"The responsibility of the contractor for insurance between fob and quay makes it impossible to..."

This is obstruction—shooting off queries which should have been checked beforehand, instead of raising and helping to solve genuine problems.

Here is an axiom: "The later the arrival of a report, the more dubious its contents." Any report that arrives three days beyond the final deadline as you leave the office for the weekend is certainly flawed. But you are the one who must spot the flaw. Teams have worked late into the night for days or weeks trying to make a better case. Don't read the details; sit back and ask yourself

"Should we do this at all?"

"What if the price of oil doubled?"

"Is all the benefit to the other company?"

and other such basic queries.

You're allowed to be skeptical of anyone who offers to do a simple job in two months' time. What does she think she's being asked to do—design the first rocket to Jupiter? It probably means that she doesn't like the job, doesn't know what to do, is aghast at the complexity of the task, wants to lend it an inordinate air of importance, and, in the long run, is not going to do it right.

Looking in from the outside, it is next to impossible to tell who are the most capable people in an organization. It is only when you work closely with people that you can see their strengths and weaknesses. Don't be obsessed with trying to make an early assessment of those you meet in other firms.

Beware the know-it-all who makes snap decisions following a one-hour meeting with a customer:

"The power broker in that firm is Ann."

"The one to watch is John. He's on the way to the top."

The humor in such hastily formed opinions is that Ann and John may disappear in a month, never to be heard from again!

"Play it by ear" is an expression used by someone who wants to impress. The implication is that she will always make the wise, correct decision. In fact, it should translate as "I don't know what to do" or "I am not going to help."

The Siege Mentality

Some managers get into a castle, pull up the drawbridge, and expect to flourish in there. They

- Never call on any aid from outside
- Make persons from headquarters unwelcome
- Have all sorts of private arrangements with staff
- Resent the authority of their superiors and try to undermine it
- Are isolated from production staff
- Become cliquish, spending too much time with the same people
- Tend to have "spies" who keep them filled in about other workers

All this goes on for a few years, but then performance falls off. The private deals do not keep the lid on staff claims. The cure is to replace such "kings" and "queens" with someone who can undo the damage.

The opposite to the siege mentality is the following type of manager:

- Adopts for her unit immediately all good ideas introduced both inside and outside the company
- Solicits and accepts all the help and advice possible from headquarters
- Meets with groups of workers regularly and discusses openly the performance of the firm
- Squeezes all possible support and work out of superiors

- Has no inside deals with anyone; everything is above board

Which type are you?

Personal Diplomacy

Avoid a condescending or dictatorial tone: "This is a very complex matter that takes days to calculate" implies that the listener may lack the cleverness and advanced education needed to understand it. Be careful.

Nor should you allow an "offended" tone to creep into your conversation: "I don't do all this work for fun, you know." Is no one entitled to query you without triggering an outburst?

In an argument, watch things like peevishly throwing down your pencil or glasses on the table. This signals an end to open discussion, and that may not be what you want. Unfortunately, such traits are largely habitual, so what can one do about them? Modify them to the best of one's ability.

Rudeness can cancel out many positive aspects of a very efficient manager. So watch your body language.

Try to speak in terms of facts:

- 15 hours
- $276.49
- "I will answer that today."
- "I will get Spud's opinion by 3:30 p.m."
- "Jane—can you get that inquiry out by next Tuesday?"

Realize that in common with every other manager, you think that

- You don't get your fair share of the company budget.
- You don't have enough staff (look at your unfilled positions—two sick, three on vacation).
- You are not allowed to offer salary incentives sufficient to attract talented new staff.
- You have a tougher job than most.

You must meet your deadlines without recourse to such excuses. It's a matter of honor—and good taste. In emergency conditions you might even have to do some work yourself! "Better late than never" is passé. The new rule is "Late is for weenies."

Confine yourself to making the errors you should be making instead of making those that should be made by your subordinates!

Human Drama in the Workplace

A reluctance to believe that anyone is malingering is healthy. A person's pride and dignity depend partly on the satisfaction derived from doing a task well. Few people will purposely do something badly. Perhaps they lack ability; perhaps they are bored; perhaps they are ill; but plain willful malingering is rare.

Seek the reason why Fawn is not pulling her weight. It may be problems off the job: illness she is trying to conceal; an alcohol or drug problem, either her own or that of a friend or family member; financial worries due to illness in the family; incompatibility with the boss. Keep an eye on supervisors who develop incompatibilities with more than one subordinate. Some people have trouble neatly separating their personal from their work worlds. And you can't just will it away.

Avoid having incompatibles working together. You will find out who is incompatible in your annual chats. It's not good enough to leave such a situation to work itself out. You would be better off leaving posts unfilled than having incompatibles together. They spend all their time scoring off each other. The greatest tragedy is when a less productive but more aggressive employee bullies someone with more ability.

Let's look at the other side of the coin. Do you feel grumpy on Monday mornings? If your son is fighting with his father, do you take it out on co-workers? Did your divorce proceedings affect your performance at work? Control yourself—your co-workers didn't cause the problem, and they shouldn't suffer because of your off-the-job problems.

The Velvet Glove

When you need to see someone in your office (and why invite them in if you don't need to see them?), be courteous. Phone up and say

"Do you have a minute?"

"Are you busy there?"

and say what the problem is—budget, new machine, whatever—implying that you are looking for help.

If you come on too abruptly, you'll come across as intimidating:

"Meet me at 11 o'clock sharp!"

"Come down at once!"

It's bad for nerves (and ulcers). Given the tone, your quarry probably doesn't expect the news to be of the best.

Avoid a pushy tone in a discussion. If you do not, your facts become suspect. If your position has merit and your facts are on the table for all to see, then why do you need a dictatorial tone? Decisions are not to be made on the timbre but on the quality of the wave shape.

Maintain a sense of balance when you discover an employee malingering. If you catch three of your charges playing cards 10 minutes after work should have begun, what do you do? Try doing something that can be told as a story around the office. Roaring at them won't have as much effect as saying something like "Want to draw me high card? If you win, you only have to make up the 10 minutes you owe." Then pick some unpleasant task for them to do if they lose. They'll get the message. If they don't, try this. "Want to draw me high card for your job?" This'll crack them up. Just make sure that if they are silly enough to play it through, you won't do worse than break even.

The Iron Fist

If you are aware, as you should be, that someone is not delivering the goods, make it perfectly clear.

How long should you wait before you lower the boom on a poor performer? Just be sure you have given every benefit of the doubt. Have patience, even when you feel irritated or justified in blowing your top. You should give plenty of warning and then an opportunity to recover. Give every chance to cooperate, to see the light. Amend your requirements slightly, if necessary, and try again. But if all else fails, lower the boom. If you don't have the guts to do so as a last resort, you may as well pack your bags. People are looking to you for leadership. Without having clear standards and enforcement of them, performance will seek the level of the standards of the next person down the chain of command.

If a manager is not doing the job (is overspending the budget, falling short of quality objectives, or is not making schedules), and tries to joke it off, ignores you, or just calmly plods along in first gear, then put your foot down. Everybody in an office setting finds out about such battles of will. They'll follow it very closely—sometimes even betting on the outcome—to see who wins. So, it's either you or him. State firmly what is wrong. Put a firm and fair deadline on its total rectification. And make it a choice between rectification and removal. Anyone worth keeping will fall into line.

Poor Performers

Poor performance can appear at any age. Some people fizzle out at 20, others at 40.

On the question of poor performers, there is an important distinction. If you have a young person of no promise, you will do yourself a favor to advise that person to look elsewhere for a job. But if you have such a person at lower-middle management level who is getting on in years, you have a problem. This person cannot easily get a job elsewhere, and your company policy may well be not to edge out such persons. If the employee is still capable of doing a day's work at a more basic level of decision making, you can at least divert the person out of the mainstream and into such responsibilities.

If you are in a no-win situation, say nothing. An example is the chap with a chip on his shoulder for the past 20 years who waylays you and gets into your office to plead that he should be on a higher pay scale. This person has switched unions, gone before ombudsmen, been heard by employment tribunals, and all have ruled against him.

Try saying nothing. After 15 minutes the complainer will say "Have you anything to say to that?" Answer "No." Perhaps another 15 minutes silence by you will bring the argument to a close. He has no case. Maybe he will realize that he is considered second rate, will grind to a halt, and go away, never to return.

Always give a poor performer a severe definite warning with a deadline for improvement before taking action.

Most difficult of all problems is the manager who makes it nearly to the top, and only then is found to be sadly lacking. In this case you may have to bestow some high-sounding title and move the person sideways where the potential for doing harm is minimized. The nearer the top, the more dangerous this disease, as it affects other people further down the line. A highly intelligent lazy person often causes this problem.

Break It to Them Gently

If you have to move someone out of a job because that person does not match the performance you need, remember, someone put him there and he may have worked in that post for some years, and to the best of his ability (however poor).

You get what you want—the move. So put some effort into moving the employee into another job more suited to his talents. For example, if someone is poor at handling people, don't send that person into a situation that demands people-handling skills.

The replacement for a person moved involuntarily must be very obviously better. Otherwise, why change? The manager who makes such a decision is in the spotlight. Everyone is watching the outcome to see if it was really an advantage to move their co-worker, and if they are going to benefit by a replacement. They all may be thinking: "I could be next."

The Troublemakers

The Backstabbers

Backstabbers are devious. They criticize the staff that works for a colleague. Mostly, the criticisms will be aimed at those reporting directly to, and who are thus closest to that colleague. The backstabber can never be accused of criticizing the colleague; that could be seen as jealousy, ambition, oneupmanship. No—she does the sly thing instead. Clearly, if all those reporting to the person targeted can be shown to be poor performers, by implication the colleague can be assumed to be a poor manager unable to motivate staff.

Indeed, the backstabbers often go further. They will even inform you—with a sly smirk—whenever one of the children of a colleague fails an exam, is on drugs, or crashes a car. Better still is to be able to point up a family member of a colleague who is involved in some scandal. Any and every opportunity to lower the status or damage the reputation of a colleague is grasped. If a close relative of a colleague is on the team reporting to the backstabber, then extra effort will be given to examining that relative's work in case it can be found second rate in any way.

Who is fooled? Not you, I hope. These are veils to be torn down. Don't hide your irritation with such behavior.

The backstabber is a mudslinger, always eager to stress the negative about work being done by colleagues or the boss:

"This new budgeting system has inflated the costs for my department."

"This new set of criteria for quality control is delaying my program and all the improvements I had planned."

"I've been fighting for years to keep down travel and entertainment expenses; Spiro and Donahue there don't seem to mind treating themselves to useless junkets to the west coast."

The backstabber tries to undermine the authority of the boss. This will be done in underhanded ways, such as

- Always running down the boss when he or she is not present. "Do you know where she was at 11 p.m. Sunday night?"
- Implying that the boss plays favorites among managers with regard to allocating funds and staff.
- Taking every opportunity to complain to the boss about the actions of other managers—without ever speaking directly to those persons.
- Saying that the boss is afraid to face down some managers.

The backstabber always tries to put the manager in an embarrassing position, never passing up a chance to pose the difficult question:

- If a sudden strike occurs at a plant, he will ask the manager "What is your timetable to fix this strike?"
- If an employee is sick for a month and the boss queries it, then the question is "Are you telling me to fire him?"

Disaster befalls any firm, or government, or council, or football team where the players are not in cooperation. This disease is common. It stems from jealousy and greed. I have seen this disease hit as follows:

- A government cabinet that argued and fought internally, resulting in their losing the next election and thus all their cabinet posts.
- Several football teams that were composed of first-class players but failed to win games.
- Companies that foundered because the management team could not agree or cooperate; it affects all sizes of companies.

It is manifested by a person who is jealous of the boss and takes every opportunity to criticize:

"I see Kermit now has use of a company car to go home from work."

"What worries me about this deal he has done is that we have nothing for California in 1989."

Stupid top managers listen and sometimes promote the jealous one to replace the other. What a disaster will follow!

Whisperers

Don't listen to rumors, whispering, or backbiting. These can appear in simple guise:

> "I'd like to warn you that so-and-so is going off bidding for a huge contract in Oklahoma without any authority."

> "Did you know that Mr. Jinxs owns controlling interest in the company that sells us all our pencils?"

As a part of office politics, there is a great temptation to create, encourage, and even cultivate the "grapevine." "Whisperers" are those who tip you off about what is going on behind your back. Especially managers who feel isolated develop a need to listen to such people and, even worse, to believe and act upon the information.

Two detrimental results derive:

- The informers, trying to ingratiate themselves with you, tend to spice things up by showing you that all others are up to some villainy, or inefficiency, or unapproved activity.

- You gradually come to believe that nothing is being done even half right.

In the long run, you will regret getting caught up in this game.

The whisperer's story is seldom entirely accurate. If it were, then the whispering would not be necessary. The whisperer would just go through routine formal channels to call attention to and alleviate the illegality, wrong, or inefficiency.

Your job, as manager, is to try to be equitable. If someone comes to you with an accusation involving a colleague, one way to deal with it is to stop the person, pick up the phone, and invite that colleague in. Then ask the plaintiff, "Now, would you like to go over that again?" This time, the accusation will probably be less harsh, more careful, and more correct. And the defendant will have a chance to respond: "How can you say I didn't make any effort to get the Houston sale. They called this morning and placed an order." Next time, your plaintiff will call the defendant (if they're still speaking) to make sure of his information, which is what he should have done in the first place instead of hurling a non-problem in your face. Those who want to impress the boss with their "concern" for the company and who are hot to "keep the boss informed" about any errors by anyone in the firm will thus be forced to get the facts or hold their fire.

Do not get out pen and paper and write a note blowing the ears off the supposed culprit. Besides, a call takes about ten seconds; a note takes longer.

Everyone will know who whispered—he's always at that. If you, as manager, mishandle such situations, you will have lost some credibility by appearing to have encouraged a spy ring, and your culpability will be no less than the people who started it all.

Don't think it's smart to be able to say, "I have my sources." If you foster whisperers, you generate in your organization

- Suspicion
- Intrigue
- Lying
- Character assassination

What a prospect!

The Magicians

If you don't believe in magic in the rest of your life, why do you believe the people who

- Claim to have landed a $200,000 order. Check to see if it has gone through the system.
- Wave letters of credit in front of your nose. Have the chief accountant check it out.
- Enjoy a life style beyond any means that you can see. A little suspicion might be in order.
- Never take a holiday, especially if it is your head accountant. Nobody loves it that much. If your head accountant never takes a holiday, you might consider going down to the local police station and having yourself arrested before someone finds out that some large swindle is going on under your jurisdiction. If you take no holidays, what swindle are you hiding? Yes—it can be the boss that is at it, and if there is a board of directors watching a firm, they should be very aware of this possibility.
- Do not allow any separate account that does not go through the full rigor of the accountancy system; otherwise, someone may milk the cow.

The Nags

Don't nag. Nagging is

"Well, why didn't you...?"

"Where are you when I need you?"

"Didn't I already tell you...?"

"Can't you do anything on your own?"

"But it's not finished..."

"I can't turn my back for a minute around here!"

Nagging is usually characterized by a state of perpetual irritability (better see a doctor). You farm-raised gents and ladies have probably seen an old hatching hen with newly hatched, helpless chicks: squak, squak, squak, cluck, cluck, cluck. Are your chicks allowed to raise a peep?

Praise and Blame

"Mol an oige is tioci si" is an old Gaelic proverb. It means praise the young and they will react favorably. Try applying it to young and old alike.

Don't be too proud to congratulate. Your skill at criticism may be well known. But can you also ease up and give credit where credit is due? It's harder to praise than blame. It lowers the differential between you and the recipient, and perhaps you fear narrowing (or reversing) the gap.

All workers think they are doing a pretty capable job (within the limitations set on them by the organization and the boss). And they genuinely do not understand why there is not a whisper of praise to reward their daily efforts. People never see themselves as lacking in judgment, or being precipitous, or stupid... It is depressing to have months of serious, dedicated, effective work upset by sudden criticism of a minor matter, with never a whisper of praise or appreciation.

Every boss should make it a routine matter of business to know important achievements immediate subordinates have made, for the purpose of making comments—and praise, if it is due. As a manager myself, I am constantly coming across excellent work, done some time back, that was not even brought to my attention at the time.

Such silence does not necessarily stem from modesty. There is often no ready way in which a subordinate can, without appearing to brag, keep you informed. Once you have established a bank of knowledge and can acknowledge excellence, not only have you established the needed channel of communication, but you are also in a better position when you need to comment critically on the one item in 10,000 that goes awry.

Ring or, better still, write (so the recipient can show it around) a congratulatory note to someone who sets you back on your heels:

To: Well Done

Subject: Budgets

Excellent

Signed: I. M. Pressed

But this is an issue that deserves examination from the opposite end as well. As you go through life, be your own judge of whether you are doing good work. You don't need anyone to tell you when you did a good job. Very often they will not say a word. The satisfaction you get is in knowing everything fell into place and that it was your doing. Don't look for any back slapping. If it happens, fine; that's a bonus. Maybe the boss is just praising you because she read somewhere that bosses should do so to motivate their staffs to do further good work. If you're going to let a dearth of praise get you down and negatively affect your performance, you'll spend the better part of your time in a huff.

Watch for any manager who habitually blames and criticizes subordinates, especially if you don't see the faults when that manager is absent, and didn't see them before he moved in. This type may be using criticism of others to shift the focus away from his own inefficiency:

"I haven't received Spock's figures."

"As usual, Scotty gave me a load of rubbish."

When was the information requested—on time, or five minutes ago?

If it is warranted, the good manager always praises staff and supports them in front of colleagues and the boss. This shows that the team is working well. If it is not warranted, she says nothing. There's no point in airing your dirty laundry for all to see.

Keep Your Cool

Never lose your cool. It is acceptable, on occasion, to be "professionally" aggressive or annoyed, or to put on a show of being so in order to get results. But if you do not return to calm at the end of the show, your bad temper will be the primary memory people take from the meeting.

If you are bad-tempered or constantly aggressive, eventually your colleagues will tire of it and stop making allowances for it. They won't bother telling you so, but you will be ostracized. They will simply cease bothering to include you in discussions.

Losing your cool shows that you have no reasoning to support your arguments. You fall back on emotionalism. Some managers get addicted to this. Having found that it worked before, they figure it is a safe bet it will work again. Do not lower yourself by such displays of lack of personal control—and wretched manners. Watch the very best managers. Do they fly off the handle?

Are you the only one in your work environment who does things correctly? If you get a complaint, do you automatically assume the complainant is right and that your staff has fouled it up once more? Are you perpetually rushing off to fix up what you see as a mess?

Perhaps the complainant has omitted to tell you some key aspects, something that might put him in a poor light. Take an example. If a phone call or letter arrives saying that a person was sold a dud machine by your firm, would you go off immediately and interview the complainant without checking with the person who sold the equipment? Imagine what happens if you agree prematurely to replace the machine. What if, in actuality, the owner drained the oil—or some other essential fluid—from the engine, forgot to refill, and ran the machine to destruction?

So look before you leap. In work, as in our system of justice, you will come out better in the long run to take the positive attitude, to presume innocence on the part of colleagues and subordinates until proven otherwise. Trust each of your staff until they give you good reason for distrust.

The Critical Many

Listeners never hear bad of themselves. But for those not there to hear, it's a different story. If you ever overhear two people talking on a plane, train, or bus, they seem invariably to be raking someone over who is not present. Similarly, at work any two persons meeting will tend, during a discussion, to agree on some shortcoming of a person not within hearing (often about their boss). This gives the two talkers a feeling of superiority in that they can both agree that this third party is some lower form of life. Ironically, when person three meets one of the other two, the one not now present is roasted in turn—and so the dance continues ad infinitum.

This practice leads each person to cultivate a rosy picture of his or her own abilities. After all, that person is the only one person never criticized in such conversations!

Remember, when you criticize a colleague, you implicitly give that person justification to criticize you in turn. So don't dish it out if you don't want it back. And most of us don't.

Occasionally the criticism gets back to the person criticized in a round-about, completely altered version: "Brenda thinks you're a lunatic. She said your plan for marketing cowboy boots in Vatican City was crazy." What Brenda really said was that she "wasn't sure the plan had been thought through as thoroughly as it might have been and that she was not too sure it would be successful." Troublemakers get a thrill out of passing back all criticism—with the author identified. Remember this.

People conveniently forget their failures and tend to glorify their successes. This makes them all the happier as they wander through life. Napoleon's tomb in Paris has recorded on it all the famous things he did, except, of course, Waterloo.

Unfortunately, others have the reverse tendency to harp on our failures, and they are irritated by our successes. As Shakespeare said, "The evil that men do lives after them, the good is oft interred with their bones."

Do not be dismayed by everyone else's glee at

- Seeing their own good work
- Noticing and remembering well all the mistakes and poor judgments on your part

Just be aware of it.

It is no skin off your nose to admit the excellence of the work of someone who is no threat to your position. "Don can sweep the floor with the best of them" is easy to say. But if a colleague or a direct subordinate does something excellent, it is harder to come out with unqualified praise—or any praise at all.

There is an old saying: "Self praise is no praise." So if anyone attempts to broadcast their own success, all that happens is that colleagues and bosses resent it and get somewhat irritated.

Management Courses

Send those with promise and good judgment to top management courses. It will repay tenfold. They will return different and better. Having a group of managers working together who have been on such courses is an advantage in that they are familiar with and up to date on the management facilities and techniques available.

Don't send persons of poor judgment and narrow vision to a top-level management course. They will lapse into a stupor within a day.

Unfortunately, they invariably retain the jargon and trot it out as proof
(1) that they were paying attention at the workshop and (2) that they
now possess top management potential.

Do in-company courses on

- Effective speaking
- Languages
- Computer literacy

Offer them immediately after normal working hours. This will eliminate those who would attend during working hours just to get away
from their desks for a change of scene.

There are some pitfalls involved in management courses. A management course is in some respects a bit of a con-trick. Take, for example,
seminars for learning about what is called your "management style."

You join the course. You fill in a chart which is then analyzed by the
lecturer. You are shown to be mainly a "Theory X" type manager. By
the end of the course, you will have learned more about management
theories. You will fill in another questionnaire. Lo and behold, it is magically proven that you have moved toward the more acceptable "Theory
Y," or "Z," or whatever brand of management the lecturer has taught as
desirable. All such exercises make it seem worthwhile to have attended
the course. I wonder how much change occurs in reality? Watch that
you don't just return to your office and resume the same old X-type
routine you've been doing all along.

Watch out for courses run by the marketing departments of com-
puter firms. It will not be sold as "Computer Course" or "How to Work
Computers." It will be billed something like "An Exclusive Course in
Communications Technology for Top Managers."

It will be addressed to company directors only and will show a list of
such groups that have already fallen for the gimmick (sorry—already
been "wise enough to attend"). "The directors of the 27th Bank of
North Wombatville attended! So why not send your top managers today!"

In a way, it's like shooting fish in a barrel. Senior managers often suffer from "computerphobia." They see all this computer equipment in
the offices of top managers in other firms. They wonder what all those
little knobs and buttons do. They feel stupid. So they would dearly like
to get in on the act. Why not sneak away for a three-day course and
learn all about it?

In practice, such courses turn out to be vague and not too detailed.
Not daring to show up the stupidity of those attending, the company

putting on the course will deal in generalities. As the three days progress, it will dawn on the participants that the person looking after the arrangements is a rep from the marketing department of the computer firm. The last session on day three will be a demonstration of all the marvelous things this firm and its products can do for yours (for a few million dollars). They will certainly get a form filled out by participants to record what help they think they will need from computers and who the rep should call on to help eliminate the desperate lack of knowledge and supposed bottlenecks that plague the computerless. In other words, you've just paid a few hundred dollars a head to someone who just wants to sell you something and conducts courses as a channel for the sales pitch.

If you can't do all that by getting your education from your own computer manager, then you are not using her correctly. Get your own expert to lecture the top directors of your company. You'll save money and will undoubtedly learn more.

The Credentials Inflation Game

The credentials of lecturers and consultants are worth a look too. I once attended a lecture on critical path analysis as part of one of these management courses. It became pretty clear pretty soon that the lecturer was out of his depth. He made gross errors in the calculations on the handouts and was unaware of some important developments in the field in recent years. He was listed in the literature as "Professor of Project Management at University of X." A letter to that institution got the response that he was not a professor really, but had been a research assistant for a year!

Such lecturers are often very good speakers, have marvelous slides, are amusing, dress well, have charm, but gee whiz...

You will hear in these lectures things like

"When I was at IBM..."

"During my tenure at AT&T..."

"At Pan Am I was working on..."

If you query these firms, you often learn some awful truths; for example, that the lecturer, working as a junior analyst with a firm called in to do some information gathering, was only there for three weeks!

Running on Empty

Don't you get fed up with presumptuous statements like

"Henry Ford had it all wrong. He forgot he was in the transportation business rather than the automobile business."

"The railroad firms were stupid. They should have expanded into transportation in general. That is why they crumbled."

"The Pneumatic Controls Company should have seen that the future lay not in pneumatics, but in controls. They should have gone for electronics."

It's all great fun, but it's nonsense. Think what is being said: Were the railroad companies, in addition to running their own very complex show, supposed to anticipate, intercept, and assume the lead in air transport and trucking? That's just not how things work. Life is not like that.

Developments come from one source—maybe in a back shed—and nobody knows it is coming or whether it will wither quickly. Insulting the memory of Henry Ford does not raise the status of the lecturer. It just sounds foolish.

What is wrong with the rise and fall of business firms? Nothing. It's like the life cycle of a person. Indeed, this is well recognized by people who observe the growth and decline of specific products in the market, so why not apply the principle to whole businesses?

A Practical Approach to Book Learning

Start with Drucker, Parkinson, *Up the Organization* by Robert Townsend, *The Peter Principle* by Dr. L. J. Peter and R. Hull, *Management and Machiavelli* by Anthony Jay, and go on from there.

Pay attention to the shelves in other managers' offices. The books that are there are a good gauge of a person's judgment. But don't take it as a rule of thumb that a person's skill in management stands in proportion to the number of such books on display in the office. A truly efficient manager would borrow them from the company library, return them when read, and recall them only when necessary. Maybe the books are there, behind the glass of the bookshelf, to impress visitors like yourself. How dusty are they? How dog-eared? (No offense to you dogs who may have picked up this book to chew on for a while.) Have you heard about the Irish wag who once offered his services to maul books for the rich so that the owners would appear to have perused all the erudite tomes on their shelves?

Reading management books is largely an exercise in self justification. The indifferent manager enjoyed *The Peter Principle* as much as the excellent manager did. Both recognized other manager types in it. Readers of management books (including this one!) nod their heads wisely as they browse, seeing themselves as the wise, balanced, far-seeing, sympathetic, supercommunicative, efficient heroes. References to the inefficient, slothful, vacillating, uncommunicative poor style are clearly seen as being directed at the villainous "others." You should know by now, though, that part of my message is to get you to realize that it may be you who is being described. But I'm taking no bets that you will get the message or will do one iota about it.

Bone up on specific skills that are needed in your job:

- Interviewing
- Staff assessment schemes
- Budgetary control
- Computer programming

You can acquire this knowledge bit by bit from the literature, or you can get it in larger doses by taking formal courses. Just make sure you're learning new skills and that you keep developing them as the years pass.

Get the best information available to enable you to do your job. The existing methods of doing the job should be in the company's files. Use that as a base. If you have no time to improve on that, then you are not using your time properly. Return to Chapter 1! Do not pass Go! Do not collect $200!

Chase information via libraries, institutions of learning, and computer data services. If you're computerized, use as much of the already-developed software as you can to perform the functions you have to perform.

When you develop a better way to do something, write it down in article form and mail it to a technical magazine for publication. Can't hurt.

Some Management Miscellany

You can spend a lot of time upholding the authority of all managers at all costs, or you can encourage everyone from junior to senior rank to work effectively to forward the aims of the company. Those who deserve encouragement from you, whatever their rank, are those who

- Work hard
- Are effective
- Get a team working well
- Are honest

And this goes for those not reporting directly to you as well.

Just Remember

Don't spend time protecting managers who are not pulling their weight. To get results, ineffective, useless, or shifty managers must be exposed. Visit them without notice occasionally when they are working with their subordinates to see how the game is being played.

It is not good management to side against subordinates with experts from outside your department. A production manager, for instance, fearing strange disciplines, may take the safe line that the experts must surely be right. Without the knowledge or mettle to debate a question, she may take sides with design, finance, personnel, sales, or public relations people against her own subordinates. She is more concerned with appeasing peers than with being a good manager, trusted and respected by her staff. There will be occasions when she has to rule in favor of outside agencies, but when a subordinate puts the issue to her, it will have to be thrashed out pretty thoroughly if it is not to have serious repercussions on the morale and productivity of the team.

People work at different speeds.

- One is the slow but sure horse who is never wrong.
- Another does the exciting job at top speed but dawdles over the dull routine.
- A third is inaccurate.

So you must manage the three in different ways. Leave the first alone, check the third daily, and program the routine for the second.

Integrity

If you say something, mean it—and then do it. Do not break a promise. Don't lie. If you start, it will snowball, and you will need a fantastic memory to keep track of all the things you've told to different people. And even if your memory is excellent, it is simply not worth the risk of being exposed as a liar. You will now have given everyone else a perfect right to lie to you.

Never take reports or letters drafted by someone else, rewrite bits, and submit it as your own work. You will undermine morale and damage your integrity. If you have some good reason for making changes, explain it to the author, and if you still disagree, add your own note and sign your addition. But leave the original unmolested and signed by the person whose work it is.

Never plagiarize. If you present a paper at a conference, let it be your own personal work. It is allowable to get information to allow you to draw conclusions of your own, but if you take work initiated by another, and because you are the boss print it under your name, you are a fraud and a thief.

It is all right to get help if you are making a speech on behalf of the firm. That is acting as a public relations representative for the firm and is not cheating on authorship.

Flattery

We all go through the world flattering our colleagues and friends on things unrelated to work:

"You couldn't possibly have a child 20 years old!"

"You are looking great. I love your hair."

Let's leave it that way.

The Funk Factor

Of all the unproductive things we do... There is a great temptation for bosses to cover their asses. They read in the newspaper of firms that fold because the higher-ups were unaware of bad contracts placed without their knowledge, or of $100,000,000 siphoned off by a head accountant. So what do they do? They become hawks, watching every turn and launching memos, the purpose of which is to keep their noses clean, not to get work done. Granted, such behavior is sometimes justifiable, but you won't spot the swindler this way (see elsewhere in this book on how to do that).

It's a difficult situation. It's hard to know where reality leaves off and paranoia begins. It leads to whispering campaigns. "Did you know...?"

"Thanks for the info." Everything rumored is believed. More memos and countermemos.

But there is a preventive method, which is to have a watertight system of automatic reporting by exception. For example

- If you don't want any orders placed in any country or for a particular type of business, set up a block on those.
- Get your auditors to check and double-check the money control system.
- Watch the lifestyle of your executives; they can't be that lucky at the racetrack.

A Final Word

"A good boss is never without good workers and a good worker is never short of a job."

Cardinal rules of Chapter 7

DO	DON'T
Judge on performance alone	Take excuses for poor performance
Promote initiators	Protect poor managers; expose them to rough weather instead
Promote heavyweights	Believe anyone who claims to be busy all the time
Sack young incompetents	Put a "demarcation" person into planning
Move older low flyers sideways	Talk too much when interviewing
Use formal assessment to pick winning employees	Promise a promotion before the interviews are held
Praise when it's due	Nag, be sarcastic, intimidate, lie, or plagiarize
Set specific duties and dates	Criticize colleagues or boss
Get all the outside help you can muster	
Have fun working	
Try an unsigned limerick to get action	

8

Career Pointers

Optimism

With all the talk of unemployment and recession, you might think chances of progressing in a career are slim. Not at all. Remember, in western countries at least, population growth has almost leveled off, so the demographics are in your favor. Also, don't forget to take into account the number of people who retire each year from the work force for other reasons—at least 3 percent. That is a quarter in eight years.

But don't pin your hopes on any one firm to provide you job security for the next 30 or 40 years. Those who claim most loudly that they will retire at 55 don't. It's too arbitrary. Maybe such people are hoping everyone will respond that they can't be done without and would they please, please stay on. Of course, nobody replies like that, so they have to linger on—58, 60, 62, 65—proclaiming their impending retirement every day along the way. The ones who actually do decide to retire early spring it on you without warning.

Rules about retirement age are comical. Bosses who at 60 have no intention of retiring until 65 are sometimes heard to berate subordinates who have been 25 years in the same job: "About time we got some new blood around here; Jenny is over the top [at 54]." It would be like the Pope, who stays on for life—80 or 90 years—laying down a new rule that bishops must move aside at 70—the prime of their youth.

Responsibility

Early in your career, try to get into a job in which you have to make decisions and in which it is just not possible to talk problems over with your boss. Try to get some distance from the boss—300 miles is a nice round number. After a while in such circumstances, you will find you can get through twice or three times the work of those people at head-quarters. Or, of course, you could become an ineffective drone. Which would you rather be? Which would you prefer everyone to think you are?

If you know the business well and know why management is failing, take the top job in the failing section and make a success of it. Never be a doormat to stupid management.

Do not take a job that you do not really want—even if it's a promotion. An example is being sent into a plant as an adviser to "improve productivity" or some other such euphemistic function. The management there is probably rotten and you would be on the wings advising a management that will not listen.

Learning

You must keep accumulating knowledge and experience suited to your profession. Your schooling was merely getting you to gain some useful basic knowledge. Why then should you cease learning at 20 or 25? If you cease to learn, then you will be outstripped by all your contemporaries.

To keep learning you can

- Keep up with the latest literature in your field

- Affiliate with a learning institution that specializes in your interests

- Take every opportunity to find out how others with jobs similar to yours go about doing it

In the business I am in, for example, it is easy to look up the annual performance of the electricity utilities and see which ones do best—and which particular power plants outperform all others year after year. A visit to such a plant is an education in itself. Indeed, it is usually not the complexity of successful operations that will strike you, but their startling simplicity.

Under the category of learning from experience, why not listen to the distilled wisdom of past generations. It may irk the young sometimes, but such wisdom was dearly earned. Take a few examples:

"A penny saved is a penny earned." It's still a penny, or a dollar, or a thousand dollars, whether it's earned or saved, and it's no more easy or difficult to do one than the other.

"A bird in the hand is worth two in the bush." If there is a quick way to solve a problem, get on with it. Don't hold off in the hope that better answers will emerge.

"Faraway hills are green." It's all too easy to envy someone else's job for the salary or the ease, but what if you were actually having to do the work involved?

"A stitch in time saves nine." Planning ahead, preventive maintenance, and the like can save a lot of headaches in the long run.

To learn fast, you must be active. For example, bring into your firm an esteemed customer and ask her to give a talk to your production, design, and sales staff on how she sees your products. If your staff stonewalls such a session and refuses to gain ideas for useful improvements, then you have reason to be very worried about the future of your business.

The Job for You

It is not very possible to effect improvements and changes until you get into a job where you can call the shots. This requires patience. You can suggest, hint, and imply, but you can't really get your ideas moving as rapidly as you would like. So work toward creating or finding a post where you are on your own and in charge, even if it means temporarily taking a less desirable schedule to get such an opportunity.

Measurability is an important aspect of any job. You must know where you stand. Take a position in which you can measure your results, so that you can take responsibility for both the good and the bad.

Enterprise is equally important. Don't shrink from taking a post where there has been a tradition of mediocrity, where previous incumbents have been "sent to Coventry." Enjoy the challenge of lifting it out of the mud.

Symbols of Status

Status symbols are not aids to decision making. Plush offices are a mockery of efficiency measures taken in a company. Remember, if you change the carpet in your office just because you don't like the color, the whole firm will remember it when you try to rouse it to cut costs and improve efficiency. An isolated group in plush offices becomes aloof. They will become involved in each other's work because they are trapped in this managers' cage. The only people they meet are colleagues of equal rank who are in charge of other parts of the business. So everyone discusses everything, but in isolation from the rest of the staff.

It is far far better to have each manager close to where the work occurs that she is supervising. The telephone makes it unnecessary to concentrate a group of managers in one place.

Incompetent persons are very keen on what they view as "status." This can include everything from having a carpet on the office floor to having a coat stand to having an office with an outside window. Some people spend half their time trying to figure out ways to attain such trappings. They are oblivious to the amusement their colleagues derive from such empty, pointless endeavor.

I recall an incident in which such a person went to the chief accountant complaining that she, a section manager, had no carpet on her office floor, whereas all the others on the same salary level had carpet. The argument kind of fizzled out when she looked down and noticed that the chief had no carpet.

Large new office blocks and suites with wall-to-wall carpet are, as Parkinson said, the signs of rot in an organization. Not knowing how to truly improve the business, the bosses go into architecture and become semipatrons of the arts.

So don't bother with the size or aspect of your office, the size of your desk, or the color of your telephone. Bother instead about how well you do your work. This is more likely to get people looking for ways to give you the trappings rather than ways to deny them to you.

Titles

Titles of positions in a firm mean little, like the titles of countries. For example, you can be fairly sure that any country called the "People's Democratic Republic" excludes the people from a free say in affairs. It is very unlikely to be democratic. As for being a republic, any country can claim that.

So it is with posts. The grand title may belie the influence of the incumbent. For example, take the grandiose title

Interdepartmental Communications Manager (mail room clerk)

Sometimes a grandiose title is invented when a person's usefulness has declined or ceased and that person is being moved to one side. Such titles look good on visiting cards and office doors.

Why do we do this? Perhaps to give a sense of worth to someone in a less responsible or less interesting position. It is fairly certain that the actual contribution of the incumbent will fall somewhat shy of the grandeur implied in the title. So don't put too much stock in the titles of others—or your own.

Promotions

Promotions occur in organizations in waves. Study the trends and see if you are in a position to ride on one of these waves. They seem to occur at about 25-year intervals. The top jobs get filled by people around 40 years of age, give or take a few years. A business that grew rapidly about 20 years ago is a good target. In about five years time, jobs will start becoming vacant. If you have shown your worth, you will be in the race. The older the firm, the more attenuated these waves are, because of different career patterns, but the wave is still to be seen.

Sometimes an applicant for a job is beaten to it by an unexpected candidate. If, when this happens, the defeated candidate turns sour, everyone will feel like justice was done. Nor will they be sympathetic when it comes to future promotions.

Ironically, such unexpected appointments tend not to stay too long. They often are fast-trackers on the way up. So a year later the job becomes vacant again. By now, though, the sour-grapes candidate, whose performance has deteriorated in the meantime, loses out again.

So if you are the defeated candidate, allow yourself a week or so to sulk. Then forget it. Turn around and prove to the boss that you are still in the running when other positions become vacant.

Do not despair if you do not get ahead as quickly as you would like. Go to your boss and ask for advice as to how best to climb the ladder. Ask what you can do in your present position to enhance your chances and how you should change your ways to get ahead, before you are set in your ways.

Tactics

Read up on interviewing techniques so that you understand just what an interviewer expects of candidates. List three or four advantages you have for the job. Be sure you don't leave the interview without having brought out these points.

Mobility

Don't stay in a job for too long, hoping that by doing it well the job will be uprated. You are expected to do it well. Nor should you start slow and work up to pace over a year or two. You will fool no one, or if you do, it will not be in the way you intended.

Independence

Paddle your own canoe. Don't try to ride your boss's coattails up the ladder. She may not move up as far or as fast as you think. Worse still, she may not retire just when you want her to, regardless of what she's said. Keep this in mind if you're beginning to see yourself as the logical successor to your superior. Don't hitch your wagon to any other.

Do not be a doormat. Don't write speeches for others to make. Don't write technical papers for others to publish under their names.

A Fair Race

Everyone has a fair race in life. If you have intelligence and ability, you can get ahead in the democratic world. There is a saying in Ireland: "No man was ever as good as his father." This is consoling in a way. It reduces the pressure on the sons and daughters of the rich and famous to follow suit, because it is by no means guaranteed, or even likely, that they will be as gifted as their famous fathers and mothers. It also reduces pressure on employers to hire on the basis of name rather than merit. It's not the oil heirs you're looking for, but intelligent young people, well educated, hard working, ready to make their own way.

Of course, if you fail, there is no end to the list of persons you can blame. But if you succeed... Well, we all know the success is owing entirely to your own talents! Shrinks make a lot of money listening to those in the first category, charging huge sums to listen sympathetically to their neurotic blaming of everyone but themselves.

You are lucky. Lots of people may be more intelligent than you, but intelligence is like natural athletic ability—unless you train and develop better skills and techniques, you will never win even on the high school level.

So if you develop the skills covered in this book, and others that you see by observing other people, then average intelligence will suffice to outpace most of your contemporaries.

In the Beginning

As a new recruit, you must, of necessity, find yourself working for a dull boss. Why? Because in accordance with the Peter Principle, many of the 50 year olds who never climbed in the organization have been left behind. One of these may be the first boss you will have to deal with. It may be frustrating. You could be forgiven for thinking that your boss is typical of all management right to the top. But if the company has promoted the right people, you must begin by seeing nothing but the worst. As stated earlier, by and large the most capable people rise to the top of organizations, judged by their on-the-job performance. This is largely independent of schooling or other outside qualifications. Obviously, to become boss of an accountancy firm you will need to be an accountant. To run an engineering firm you will most likely need to be an engineer. Obviously, too, you will find exceptions.

You hear engineers complain at their professional meetings: "How can we improve the image of engineers so they get the top jobs in industry?" They are debating the wrong topic. A more useful question would be "Why are the smarter kids not choosing engineering as a career?"

Hopefully creed, color, and sex will diminish as determining factors in the future of hiring and promotion.

Bluffers and incompetents will eventually be found out. Be patient. Do not be distraught when one bluffer seems to get ahead. Put your head down and keep doing your best.

If you don't have the qualities, courage, and durability to get to the top, then you will rise to a level commensurate with your ability. If Peter is right, you go one level above that and stop there at the level of your incompetence. None of us likes to contemplate that. We prefer to think we still have a jump or two further to go!

Decisiveness

In a new post, it is totally unnecessary to overlap by more than a day or two with the departing incumbent. You're probably confident enough to feel that you are going to improve things anyway, and if the person is going further up the ladder or retiring, he or she will still be accessible by phone if necessary. To be nominated to take over months before the due date is of little use, you won't be able to make decisions until you are in the saddle.

Escapism

If you are not competent or qualified to do your job properly, you will tend to go off doing peripheral, unnecessary things such as

- Forming committees to examine what you term "cross functional" matters.
- Having several departments doing the same job so that you get two or three answers to every problem. If all answers concur, you are happy and confident. If they do not concur, you form another committee to investigate the reasons and arrive at a perfect solution (good luck).
- Hiring consultants to report to you on all sorts of topics. You assure everyone that this is no slight on the abilities of your own staff, that it is to prove to outsiders that an independent examination will vindicate your present policies.
- Centralizing—or decentralizing—authority.

A favorite escape tactic involves getting keenly interested in the filing system, or coding system for the telephone directory, and spending a year devising a complicated method for redoing it. Usually, the resulting scheme is too intricate and convoluted to be of use. Don't fall in love with your files. It's distressing to see these super-bureaucrats walking around clutching a bulky load of files lovingly to their chests.

Lame Excuses

Excuses like

"He is getting on my nerves."

"She is very grumpy."

won't get you far in the work world. Personality traits do not matter unless they interfere with output.

Don't believe that your image or reputation for infallibility must go forever untarnished; you'll never complete the course. Some bumping is inevitable. If you try to row a boat from New York to Boston without getting wet, you'll never get beyond the mouth of the Hudson.

Experience

No matter how many books you read, you cannot succeed without actual experience.

- Try to ride a bicycle for the first time, having read a book on the subject.
- Study all the books by all the recent winners of the PGA. Now go out

there and shoot par first time.

Take a look in the CEO's office. How many books do you see that are actually needed to do the job? The bicycle is being expertly ridden without written instructions.

Each new generation has to relearn for itself. Much of the practical experience a person accumulates retires or dies with that person. All the things seen and tried—but not recorded—are lost. It is frustrating to consider that the same mistakes are made over and over—even though recorded in many documents. A simple example: A keyway cut with square corners will lead to cracks and consequent failure when used on machinery. This was well appreciated 50 years ago, and 25 years ago, and is well known to-day. But it is still done. Undoubtedly, computer-aided design will in future have programs to help avoid such bad practice, but until then (and possibly afterwards—someone has to program the computer), it will still occur.

Companies that know how to avoid failure are unlikely to let their competitors know how to do so. Thus many useful tips and solutions to problems do not become generally appreciated.

Copy Cat

How do you get experience quickly? That's easy. Look at how others do it. Question them about it. Copy them with confidence. Do not attempt to work out for yourself ab initio the answers to all your problems.

Copy the good ideas of others. After all, what was your schooling but pumping the knowledge of others into your brain? You cannot possibly reinvent everything and every process again in our own lifetime. There is not time for everyone—except Missourians, of course—to be shown everything. Look at the pyramids in Egypt or the coliseum in Rome if you want to feel humble. Could you design and construct one of these from scratch?

People love to be asked how they did something, why they did it, what problems they had, and how they solved them. Take an example: I visited a utility in the United States to see how they built their power stations. I was met by the chief engineer who said "Why did you come all this way?"

"To see what sort of station we should build," I replied.

"Well," he said, "I can tell you now without putting you to the trouble of asking any more. You should build 300-megawatt units with a pressure of 2500 pounds per square inch, using natural circulation boilers," said he.

"I guess we can go home then," I replied, "because my colleague here and I intend to do just that. But can you show us yours?"

"No," said he, "I was not allowed to do the right thing. We are compelled to buy the cheapest bid without regard to quality. The professors and consultants have both convinced our board that units of 900 megawatts, high pressure, and forced circulation are the modern, efficient solution. The performance of our plant is seen as mediocre."

In a Dublin shoe repair shop is a notice: *There is nothing that can't be done a little cheaper, and a little worse.* Remember that.

But consider, if you look at what 20 other good plant superintendents do and just copy the good points, there is quite a chance that you may rival the best of them, without having to generate a single novel idea of your own.

Also, you should look at the bad results as well as the good before you decide. If you are buying a large boiler plant and a good bid comes from a firm with a list of similar plants, go and look at one or two of those recommended by the manufacturers. But beware; they will have chosen their best performers to show you. Do a little research. Look up the actual results in all plants built by this firm in the past ten or fifteen years. Choose the two worst ones, the ones that have given bad results for some consecutive years. Go and visit those plants.

Do not allow any of the maker's people to accompany you or make any arrangements for your visit to any plant. If one turns up uninvited, politely explain that the information will be more convincing to you if you go alone. Ask him to please let you see for yourself.

One large boiler firm was appalled at such a move and blamed the sales director for allowing the potential buyer to visit such a plant. It was threatened that he would lose his job unless he got this order.

As it turned out, the visit proved that all the flaws had been cleverly rectified over the preceding three years and that the new design avoided all the deficiencies. The order was duly obtained and a year or two later the real story was told. Remember, you want to buy from firms that have encountered the problems and solved them fully and convincingly. You do not want to buy from "beginner" firms building their first unit of the type and size you need. If you do, you will be sorry.

The antithesis of this attitude is where people refuse to listen and learn. They foolishly pretend that they know it all. The experience of others is irrelevant. Some companies carry this attitude to extremes and the results show it. Some whole nations suffer this disease to an advanced degree and are slowly declining. They cannot appreciate that there may be something to learn from the Texans, the Irish, or the Chinese.

Some are too proud to learn and will even prevent their staff from going to ask from others. But the Japanese and Irish do it, so why not you? There was one utility in the United States that asked us what we found worth copying from a utility in a neighboring country. They could not go and ask themselves, lest they find a technology superior to their own. Swallow your pride. Ask, look, and learn.

Work Hard

Don't be ashamed to like working. There is much to commend the Protestant work ethic. It may have gone out of fashion for some people. You don't have to be as extreme as one friend of mine who claims his weekends are boring because he loves his work so much! It is pretty aimless, though, to go through life as a drone. Why live at all if that's all there is?

Don't think you won't be noticed if you are

- Efficient
- Lazy
- Working well
- Dodging the column

Those casual supervisors notice all, but they hold their council in case you change—for better or worse—before a promotion comes along.

Personality Quirks

You must try to minimize personality quirks. Admittedly, such quirks are often a symptom of a disease you do not know you have, and which will thus be difficult to cure. Nobody will ever point them out to you.

For example, some have an exaggerated idea of their influence on affairs. Each likes to think that he or she is the one that matters. There are sales representatives who think that because they passed through Dallas five years ago, they are the reason the firm landed a huge order there last week. They think they are the catalyst that leads to all future success. This kind of egotism, however annoying, is at least tolerable if the person in question performs fairly well. It's when you see it in a poor performer, who has absolutely no reason for egotism, that it's such a tragedy.

"Mysterious" people are a menace. They wander around. Nobody can quite explain what they do. Nor is it clear what they mean whenever they speak up. Their purpose is vague and they are frequently intent on something that is tangential to the work of the section.

The complainer-moaners tell you that nobody gives them decent work to do. The perfect match here is the boss who says that nothing assigned is ever done properly. The solution: Move the complainer once. If the new boss develops the same opinion as the old boss, then tell the moaner the facts.

Do not argue. By this I mean

- Objecting to everything
- Saying no without thinking
- Being an advocate against all causes
- Raising your voice when discussing a topic

If you want to argue, become a lawyer.

Beware of anyone with a conspiratorial tone of voice, as if great secrets are being divulged.

Past glory—or near glory—overcomes many people. Bennie seizes every opportunity to trot out his story: "I once almost sold a vacuum cleaner to Elvis's maid. It was a trip." After a dozen or so recitations, everyone has learned to spot the signs that Bennie is warming up to his story. Watch them flee. Annual sales meetings are the perfect forum for this type of personality.

Some people cannot resist turning any situation into an occasion for a lecture. Writing long memos is another form of the same quirk.

Sometimes a boss is turned off by a particular subordinate. A personality quirk can cause this. The subordinate concerned may be of average or above-average ability, but the boss cannot see through her quirk and only sees what she does wrong. Every time they meet or talk on the phone, the boss is wriggling with impatience.

It requires discipline of mind to be fair to such people. Be careful not to write someone off too hastily. People can frequently be very highly motivated, and with a little attention and grooming, can turn out to be assets. If you do not grant the benefit of the doubt, you may drive out of the organization a talent that other people recognize and use—and just because you were irked.

Try to cut out speech mannerisms. Mannerisms are not recognized by the user, but they are distracting to the audience. These frequently are poorly disguised ways to monopolize a conversation. Have you ever engaged in conversation with the person who stops midsentence to light a cigarette or sip a drink or pick lint off your lapel? If their story is entertaining, you are anxious to hear the rest. If it is horribly boring, you want it to end so you can interject an excuse to leave. The thing about irritating mannerisms of speech is that the speaker may have talents unrelated to speech or tidiness that are obscured by these torturous habits.

Don't be scared that someone else will make a sensible contribution to a discussion. I've known individuals who continually utter noises just to hold the floor, or who repeat words two or three times while they're figuring out what they want to say next.

Examples of phrases used to hold the floor are

"On the other hand"

"The point is"

"You know"

"I mean"

"In actual fact"

"Sort of"

"Nicht wahr" (for Germans)

"Um...um"

Watch politicians. They are superbores. They can prevent anyone from interrupting them. They never end at the end of a sentence. They draw breath in the middle of a sentence so that they can go on forever putting forward their theories. Do *not* copy them.

Think Twice—Be Nice

Be very slow to score off people; it is too easy. You know the type who excuses insulting remarks, vicious attacks, bad-tempered outbursts, by professing to be honest: "I just say what I think." She is not a cunning, plotting, prevaricating schemer like the rest of us. It would be interesting to lock up a half-dozen of these specimens together in a room for a day.

Remember, no one is so perfect as to have no oddities or Achilles' heel or oversensitivities. You will occasionally be surprised by this, but let it be. With patience and memory you may be able to avoid some difficult situations, but it is better to operate as if you were dealing with persons of perfection. After all, you don't realize your own oddities—if you did, you would alter your style.

If you ever have to appear in public or on television, get a colleague to act the devil's advocate. Get her to try to tear you to pieces. Do the same before going to a conciliation court. You will find that only 75 percent of the potential attack will evolve and you're on an easy wicket. In this way, when you have the actual interview, you will be quite relaxed. You must write down three or four things you want to have said, and you must say these things, no matter how the interviewer tries to deflect you. Have the items on a small card that you can place in your view (but out of sight of the cameras) so that you do not miss one of your key points.

Nothing New

In 1927 Mrs. Blanche Green, reputedly the highest salaried woman in the United States, laid down some commandments for career success.

- Learn all there is to know about your job
- Be dependable in emergencies
- Be punctual
- Do not argue
- Remember that human beings are hungry for sympathy and kindness
- Do not leave your job to go into business for yourself until you are sure of your experience and your backing

It is coincidental, but in many ways my own admonishments parallel those of Mrs. Green. And in any case, it is interesting to see that many of the values and precepts we preach have remained the same over the years.

Cardinal rules of Chapter 8

DO	DON'T
Get responsibility early	Bother about status
Copy successful performers	Hitch your wagon to someone else
Get on a promotion "wave"	Read too many books on theory
Work hard	Cling to personality quirks
Enjoy your work	Hog the conversation

9

Epilogue: So What's It All About?

That problem: Do something about it NOW—not tomorrow.

Operate from the basis given in this book. You're human, so you'll have to break a rule now and then. But on the whole it is a pretty efficient base from which to start.

Don't think everything here applies to other jobs and not to yours. If you do, you've wasted your time and your money (if you didn't borrow the book from a library). I can just hear you saying: "Ah, but he never had a job like mine, with all my problems." You think not?

Much of what is written here cannot be applied in your first month at work. But a good deal of it can. When you have been five years at work, you should be able to apply 50 percent of it. By the time you retire, you can curse yourself for never using the rest.

On the other hand, don't think that I myself practice all that I recommend. In fact, I am often in astonished admiration of my colleagues in their performance under some of these headings. I fail on many.

To each of my colleagues: I hope you don't think you are the one person I was thinking about when I wrote this. All the characters are imaginary.

Don't lose heart. In 0.001 percent of cases, top managers come from those who do not do one single thing advocated in this book. One method is to marry into the owner's family.

Do not tell any of your friends about this book. After all, you have now got a lot of useful information that could give you an advantage over them in getting ahead. That's more important than gaining royalties for me. Good hunting.

About the Author

Al Kelly is director of engineering for the national electric utility of Ireland and chairman of the board of their international consulting business. He has done management consulting and has worked on technical projects for various companies around the world, including General Electric, Babcock and Wilcox, and Foster Wheeler. His book *What to Do (and What Not to Do) to Make Life Easier for Yourself at Work* (McGraw-Hill, Maidenhead, 1973) was a best-seller in three languages, and he has written dozens of articles on management and engineering. Kelly is in the *Guinness Book of World Records* for constructing the world's highest siphon.

Index